TIME PAST. . . TIME PRESENT

Essays, Stories, & Reminiscences
of What I Learned
the First Time Around

TIME PAST. . . TIME PRESENT

Essays, Stories, & Reminiscences
of What I Learned
the First Time Around

Mark Allen North

Fresh Ink Group
Roanoke

TIME PAST. . . TIME PRESENT
Essays, Stories, & Reminiscences
of What I Learned the First Time Around

Fresh Ink Group
An Imprint of:
The Fresh Ink Group, LLC
PO Box 525
Roanoke, TX 76262
Email: info@FreshInkGroup.com
www.FreshInkGroup.com

Edition 1.0 2017

Edited by Beem Weeks / FIG

Book design by Ann E. Stewart / FIG

Cover design by Stephen Geez / FIG

Cataloging-in-Publication Recommendations:
BIO000000 **BIOGRAPHY & AUTOBIOGRAPHY** / General
BIO026000 **BIOGRAPHY & AUTOBIOGRAPHY** / Personal Memoirs
BIO002000 **BIOGRAPHY & AUTOBIOGRAPHY** / Cultural Heritage

Library of Congress Control Number: 2017934566

Hardcover ISBN-13: 978-1-936442-64-5
Soft-cover ISBN-13: 978-1-936442-65-2
Ebook ISBN-13: 978-1-936442-66-9

Acknowledgements

Thanks to the following noteworthy souls:

Ann E. Stewart, managing director, Fresh Ink Group, for your direction and for seeing the whole picture. Thanks for keeping things moving.

Stephen Geez, mentor, counselor, cover designer, and more at Fresh Ink Group. Thanks for championing this work from the day it was a rough outline.

Beem Weeks, editor and social-media director at Fresh Ink Group. Thanks for pounding the prose into shape, then smoothing it to match my narrative voice, and for promoting my work.

LeAnne Wilson, literary agent, Mark North Enterprises. Thank you for your attention to details, publishing advice, and stewardship.

Milton D. Redick, Thomas P. Redick, Gay Lynn Cookson, The Wagners, and **Wilma Cradit Wood.** Your financial support and literary skills helped transform my manuscript into a book that can be understood and, I hope, embraced.

Steve Leith; Mike Clark; Dave Duyst, Sr.; and the Rasmussens. Your support for both me and this project helped me realize my dream.

Table of Contents

INTRODUCTION

INTRODUCTION

As I look back from my 80th year at the exciting experiences and ongoing mysteries of my life, I feel compelled to share a few of these stories. These reminiscences and commentaries originate primarily in Michigan, but some arise from my travels coast to coast, from Canada to Mexico, and to many islands in the Caribbean. I draw from my childhood living and working on farms, serving as an officer in the military, and having that rare opportunity at the Bendix Aerospace Division to work on the Apollo Mission while attending the University of Michigan.

I have been fortunate in many ways. Besides good health, one aspect of my life really stands out: I've had loving and caring parents, brothers, friends, and other relatives who helped me in my journey through life's foibles. A late bloomer, I started reading seriously and writing later in life. My first project was a brief memoir for my children. While many writers endure stressful, hectic, even drug-dependent lives and still write very well; I don't suffer like that, yet I struggle to write at their level. I'm still developing my skills in both non-fiction and fiction, especially action/adventure.

Please keep this in mind as you read my stories. I'm writing from the heart, and thinking of the people who have meant so much to me over a lifetime. Thanks to Fresh Ink Group and to all of you for giving me this chance to share.

THE ICE CHEST

An Essay

My formative years, from 1937 to 1950, were lived in the small downriver community of Allen Park, Michigan. Brothers Milt, Dave, and I explored the town and surrounding farms on foot, bike, and, when required, took the bus and streetcar to events out of town. We owned a car, a neat '40 Ford, but Dad drove it to work in Detroit and seldom used it on weekends due to gas and tire rationing during World War II. However, postwar travel was exciting; we were 'on the road' every possible opportunity.

Partially due to the previously mentioned rationing, many of the deliverymen used horse-drawn wagons or carriages for their milk, bread, or ice routes. We were fortunate to have one of the best ice deliverymen in Ben and his horse Old Bess. I should mention that part of the reason for many house deliveries was that all the vendors were local, most within a mile of the house. Likewise, that's the reason salesmen could make calls on foot. Also, this was the 1940s. There weren't any of the one-stop supermarkets or box stores like Walmart in existence.

In those days, shoppers scurried between the meat market, milk depot, bakery, and farmers market for groceries. House-wives, like my mother, frequently went by 'shanks mare' pulling a wheeled cart, or sent us boys to fetch goods on our bikes. That was indeed a pleasure since the store owner generally gave us a treat for our patronage.

During this time, many salesmen also walked the streets of our town. An example would be the Fuller Brush man, who had many gadgets besides brushes. He always called on Mom during the day, whereas the World Book Encyclopedia salesman came late in the afternoon when Dad would be home. There were others as well, with all sorts of labor-saving ideas packed inside their large brief-cases. One thing was certain: they all dressed in suits and ties, their heads topped with exquisite fedoras. In fact, Dad always wore a hat to church, and Mom sported a hat with a sheer veil. Times certainly have changed. Today, jeans and short-sleeved shirts seem to be the common church-going apparel. I haven't seen a woman's hat and veil in fifty years.

We all had assigned jobs around the house—mine being the care of the ice chest. Waiting for the ice man, who came twice a week, was the highlight of my day. I was tuned to hear the *clomp-clomp-clomp* of Old Bess first thing in the morning. That sound was music to my ears. My job, as the youngest, was to keep the wood cabinet clean on the outside and inside, and to daily empty the drain pan underneath. By the time I did so, on the morning of delivery I'd hear Ben saying, "Whoa…Bess." I'd spring out of the side door, prop it open, and run to greet Ben and Bess in front of our house.

Ben was a large, muscular guy, built like a bull, with massive arms. He'd been about fifty years old with snow white hair and a beard that recalled Santa Claus. Ben's uniform consisted of white bib-type overalls, a long-sleeved white shirt, and a white cap emblazoned with the *Sealtest Dairy* name atop his curly-haired head. Though Ben looked tough, he had a gentleman's heart of gold.

The wagon was white, fully enclosed with an open driving position up front where the reins of the horse passed through, and two large doors in the rear. The colorful red-spoked wheels rode on solid rubber tires.

Bess was a beautiful white and dappled gray mare with braided mane and tail and contrasting black hooves. Ben guessed her to be about ten years old, having the classic lines of a well-bred Percheron. He always said—tongue in cheek—that he chose a horse that was close to the color of the wagon. Truth was, Ben had several horses to share the work load. One thing was certain, all the horses shared Ben's friendly personality.

I received my expected "Hi!" from Ben as he opened the rear door. He always said the same thing each time: "Let's get to work." While he rinsed the sawdust off the ice, measured and scored it to the size we needed, I grabbed the curry comb and curried Bess's coat and fed her the carrot she'd come to expect.

I loved that gal. Her muzzle was soft with sparse tender hairs, and rubbery lips seemed to speak to me in a manner of saying, "Thanks." I will always wonder if she liked me as much as I liked her. I had a feeling her eyes spoke volumes of knowing who I was each morning we met. My hugs around her massive neck must have told her how much I liked her. I soon learned a lesson in life from her: If you treat an animal with kindness you will be treated the same in return.

With a quick rap, a forty-pound piece of ice split off the larger block and was ready for delivery. By this time, several neighborhood kids surrounded the wagon, looking for slivers and chunks of ice that fell off as Ben worked his chisel. We all sucked on ice in the summer as a treat almost equal to the rare ice cream cone we'd get once a month. We even enjoyed the ice in winter.

Next, Ben would position a leather pad over his shoulder, grab ice tongs, hook into the block, spin around, and throw the block onto his shoulder. Then he'd holler, "Look out, I'm on my way." I'd dash ahead to make sure the side door was still open, then run into the kitchen to open the ice chest door.

He'd swing the block into the galvanized portion of the box, and after a quick adjustment to ensure the block was right, Ben would say to Mom, "There you go, ready for another couple of days!" Mom would reply, "Thanks, Ben. See you in a few days." Ben would tousle my hair with his huge hand, thank me for helping out, and be on his way. "Up Bess," he'd say, followed by that familiar *clomp-clomp-clomp.*

For those who have never seen the beauty of an ice chest—or cabinet, as some say—it is the most elegant piece of furniture in the kitchen. Its hardwood oak panels, brass fittings of latches and hinges, ornate feet, and rich finish, stood out as a prized possession in every kitchen in the 40s. To measure its place of importance, Mom had a large doily on top with a fruit basket in its center. Some of you may know, in our current measure of collectables, it is at the top of the list.

As we all know too well, technology changes our way of doing things. This was true for our fine ice chest. It lost its job.

After the war, we purchased an ugly, electric refrigerator with the compressor element shaking on top, and the elegant ice chest was relegated to the garage to store fruits, vegetables, and other perishables, keeping them from rodents. The new *frig* was nice since it could keep ice cream in its freezer compartment, but it did cost more to operate and had to be defrosted every couple of weeks.

Then, much to my surprise, Dad realized his mistake, and moved the chest to the dining room to store dishes and glassware. Thank goodness!

True, I could no longer chat with Ben and Bess, but resolved that the experience had taught me many lessons. As some have stated, "Maybe it takes a community to raise a child." In this case, I had been fortunate to know Ben and Bess.

Home delivery gradually disappeared after the war, and without gas or tire rationing, we picked up our own groceries.

I know, change is part of growing older. But I still miss Ben messing with my hair as I helped him with the ice, and Bess's soft muzzle and tender lips taking a carrot from my hands. And I'll never forget that signature *clomp-clomp-clomp* at dawn's early light.

BOY SCOUT CAMP

An Essay

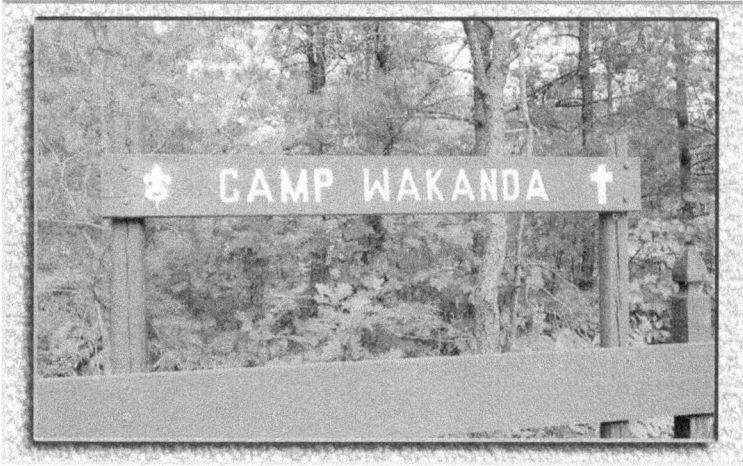

As I headed north one autumn with my first love, my thoughts wandered to the emotional ties I've long had to my favorite spot in Northern Michigan, the Presbyterian Church Boy Scout Camp called *Wakanda*, (Great Spirit).

Call me fickle, emotional to a fault, or overly sensitive to this shrine in the woods. . . all of the above could be true. Still, one thing is for sure: the objectives of scouting and its leaders transformed me from a confused young boy to a clear-thinking young man. My experiences with fellow Scouts and outstanding mentors gave me an appreciation for the wonders of Nature and, yes, the values we learned, such as doing our best, doing our duty, and obeying the Scout law, which includes being brave, clean, and reverent. As I grew older, I discovered many parallels with our nation's military values: Duty, Honor, and Country. You might notice I sound like I'm talking as if camp were a life-changing experience. It truly was.

As we continued motoring northward with the top down in our neat '58 Chevy convertible, the broadleaf deciduous oaks and maples prevalent in the southern part of the Lower Peninsula gradually gave way to the dominating evergreen pine forests of upper Michigan, a transformation that grew quite pronounced by the time we passed Houghton Lake.

There it is. . . Do you hear it?

I asked my girl if she heard the musical harmonics of pine needles telegraphing the presence of big timber.

Do you hear that, too?

She looked at me, obviously puzzled.

The thrum of wind-plucked power lines echoed across the roadway.

Look at 'em. It's '58 and the power company still hasn't updated the low-voltage wires. You might say they are telegraphing their presence.

She gave me one of those looks. I thought, not to worry, she'll give me many more of those looks before this day is over.

At the 175-mile marker the old bottle fence marked our turn-off to Old State Road. Yes, wine bottles cast in concrete, lying in a rather attractive pattern. . . Who? Why? When? Who knows? I do know many visitors have had their pictures taken with this unusual monument to the fermented grape.

How many times had the senior Scouts leaned out the window and yelled, "We're here! There's the fence!" The tenderfoot Scouts would look at each other, puzzled. They would know what it meant soon enough.

On the twenty-mile trek down Old State Road, the senior Scouts would review camp activities, including the charge that in the next fourteen days each tenderfoot was expected to earn at least ten merit badges, participate in a fourteen-mile hike, sleep overnight under the stars—that's right, no tent—plus learn and act out many of the Native American cultural lifestyles.

Someone always asked about the local black bears. "Your scout leader will be staying up all night," the senior Scout would explain. "And most of you will be staying up all night with him, watching billions of stars, some shooting across the sky." The pitch black of the area with no light pollution always surprised the Scouts. Many wanted to repeat the all-night vigil for that experience alone, or to listen again to the unfamiliar night sounds of the forest, or maybe repeat the wonder of those shooting stars, or of course to listen again to the endless stories of the leader. One Scout, not yet satisfied with his safety, was told a true story about the casual bear encounter one night during a previous trip. The leader simply barked at the bear, and it high-tailed it back into the woods. You just have to know: Bears *hate* dogs.

"Who was that leader?" they wondered. "Is he still here?"

"Yeah," someone said, easing their fears. "Frank is still here to share his forest-survival skills and, for that matter, his overall life skills that you young men can use to navigate the ever-more-complex worlds where you'll live." Frank would explain the advantages of a "buddy system," both at camp and in life. We'd all discover how important it is to have someone who can help shoulder the burdens of life's challenges and traumas, a buddy who is always available, the one you can count on for support, especially during those times when we're in survival mode. A good buddy system enhances the troop, especially as scouts discover how numbers count when performing difficult assignments. One tenderfoot pointed out that with a buddy around, he might spot a bear when you can't see it. Comments like that often led to good Q&A sessions.

As the odometer rolled over at twenty miles, that wooden arched gateway appeared on our left. *Wakanda* was spelled out with smaller white birch sticks in the arch. It looked beautiful. We stopped to absorb its splendor.

I don't know all the details about the camp's history, but I can say its 160 acres were purchased by several hunters from the state in the early '30s. This group, I believe, after years of hunting, decided to sell it to the church in the '40s. The trustees bought the property and granted the group continued hunting rights in November, and allowed them to keep their small cabin in the woods. El Lake, which is shaped like a figure 8, rests in the middle of the acreage. Its northern half is clear and deep, while its southern section is swampy and teeming with pike.

Since we were visiting in October, we assumed the camp would be empty. Sure enough, as we broke over the crest of the hill above the camp, it glowed in the noonday sun, its white clapboard cabins standing alone, not a soul around.

"Are you sure it's okay to walk around?" my girlfriend asked.

"Yep. If anyone asks, I have an answer. Our family not only camped here several years in the late '40s, but my dad was scoutmaster and our parents were some of the founding members of the church in 1932."

As I put the top up, she wondered why. I told her that if I didn't, the car would be full of acorns, pine needles, and maybe even a few squirrels.

My heart was skipping beats as we walked around the large central dining hall and small leaders cabin, then angled up a small knoll to check out six smaller cabins with bunk beds—four Scouts each—and finally the "opulent" three-hole privy next to the garbage dump that tenderfoots had to cover with earth every night to prevent odors from enticing local bears. The swimming hole was down on the north end of the lake at the end of an old lumbering railroad grade. The ceremonial fire pit sat to the south of the dining hall on an old concrete base, probably from a burnt-out cabin of the past.

The ball diamond looked well used, as if it had hosted a lot of games in the summer. I recalled how on any given evening many of us gathered on this primitive diamond. We'd choose up sides, tenderfoots playing with senior Scouts. We had no real bases, just burlap sacks, and no bases on balls—three strikes, and you were out. Sliding on Mother Earth risked getting a "raspberry" on your butt, and bragging rights went to the team in front when the game was called on account of darkness or chow. No coaches, no umpires, no scoreboard, no parents, no pressure—just the joy of playing the game of skill within a common set of rules. I couldn't help but reflect, Little League could never replicate this experience. We headed to the edge of the lake and found the stairs leading down to the boat dock, which showed the wear from generations of young feet.

We sat on that dock and dangled our feet in the cool water for a bit, drinking in the sights of autumnal color. Fallen trees littered the water's edge with their trunks, part of that eternal cycle of life, the rhythm of decay and rebirth and death.

In the decade of my absence the changes to the shoreline are dramatic, yet still somehow unchanged as the pines, oaks, and spruces continue to gather as they have for millennia.

"Look closely, dear. As the waves lap around the fallen timber, there is no sign of human activity, no manmade trash or other pollution. Our responsibility is to keep it that way, not only for us, but for our children and future Scouts."

She sighed. "How true, my dear."

That gave me an idea, so we walked down the railroad bed to the swimming beach where my promise that no one could possibly see us here so I would try to convince her to join me in skinny-dipping.

My gal was a good listener while I related stories of tenderfoots standing in the moonlight, yelling "Here, snipe! Here, snipe!" with a potato in a burlap sack; or going next door—a mile away—to get pigeon milk from the local hermit who, by the way, we're told escaped the WWII draft by hiding in the woods. I told her about the day I was caught killing frogs for baked frogs' legs, then finding out that wasn't allowed, the resulting kangaroo court making me pull cattails near the swimming area for four hours. For sneaking out one night to view the stars, I had to peel potatoes on KP for two days. As Dad used to say, "Live and learn."

Check this out: Because *Wakanda* was primitive, everyone knew the refrigeration and cooking was done by LP gas, and we needed flashlights or lanterns to see at night; but many times just before going to bed, a senior Scout would tell a tenderfoot to go to the privy and turn out the lights because someone must have left them on. More often than not, the naïve young lad would go. He might be the same fellow who'd ask where the showers are. He'd soon learn that the shower was the lake.

Hungry? Go fish. Want a treat? Pick some blueberries and the cook would gladly make a pie. Still wanting a snack? Wait for candy bar formation every other day. All candy bars were five cents, this being back when bread was ten cents a loaf.

Feeling a strong urge to check out my cabin, I convinced my gal to walk with me to look around *Patton*. She was curious about the name until we arrived at the line of cabins all named after WWII leaders, including Admiral Halsey, Admiral Nimitz, General Eisenhower, General Bradley, and General MacArthur. Figuring the door would be locked, I tried anyway, then settled for walking around and looking in the windows, even as I recalled all the tricks we would play on each other. My favorite was putting a garter snake in cousin Bill's sleeping bag. Upset, he was, despite our explaining the counselors had assured us it wasn't poisonous. That wasn't the point Bill was trying to make.

Ah, look. Come around. I found it: my Indian name, still visible on the listing of all Scouts who stayed in Patton. *To the left—do you see it?*

Sure enough, that made my day. It validated my stories—my memories—of camp.

There it is: "Walks With Wind," which in Odawa language is "Nodin Bemose."

Say, I've an Indian name for you, too. You're beautiful, svelte, cunning, and wise. It's obvious, dear: "Coyote Woman."

She smiled and said she loved it. Still, maybe I was lingering by the cabin or looking a little dejected. In any event, being so wise she sensed my feelings and said in a sexy voice, "Sorry you can't go inside and relive your past. How about me making it up to you by having you be with me tonight? You might forget *Patton*—for a moment, anyway."

After that, we walked hand in hand to the car which, as expected, was covered with pine needles and squirrel tracks.

One more stop. There should be a wigwam—a bark-covered hut—near the fire pit.

Come on. It will only take a minute.

It was here that our leaders explained that the brotherhood of scouting had its roots in the culture and organization of the tribe. There were rules with clear rewards and punishments, a buddy system, and a reverence for Nature, to name a few. Scouting taught me to follow many of these rules, or there would be consequences. Likewise, if an individual Scout needed support, the pack was there to help. I received my name here, which was based on my urge to walk everywhere and sail the camp's sailboats whenever possible.

Coyote Woman reminded me that we must be going, and I agreed.

Then I thought of one more place I had to visit.

She insisted we must be going.

I more than want to show you. I want you to feel *this place. Come on!*

Arm in arm we walked the hundred yards over a small knoll to look down on a clearing in the woods that resembled a cathedral in the pines. It had simple bench seats, plus a small lectern to the east and one to the west.

"That's a curious layout," she mentioned.

You see, we held services at sunrise and sunset. Frank gave

many challenging homilies over the years. His message was always direct and to the point on one of the several problems of young men moving into manhood. With agnostics, atheists, Unitarians, Trinitarians, and animists among the Scouts, he urged each of us to examine whether or not his beliefs made him a better person. If those beliefs required blind faith, accepting mythical doctrines such as the supernatural aspects of Trinitarianism or Native American animism, then go for it—but only if they enhanced a spiritual relationship to oneself and one's fellow men. The world being pluralistic, he taught to all beliefs. That got him into trouble a few times, but no one dared challenge that he might not be right. Frank loved *some* of Jesus' pronouncements found in the *Bible*, but rejected how the scribes "packaged" their leader. I learned a lot here as a young man, and with the guidance of Frank and the other counselors, I consider myself very fortunate.

Yes, he ruffled some feathers when he proposed that one's faith must pass the test of reasonableness rather than relying on blind biblical textualism. "It's your decision," he acknowledged. "We all have 'free will' to choose." I heard that more than once in my youth. You see, Frank was my dad.

Many ask, "Why explore the limits of our world? Why learn other cultures—examine other spiritual beliefs—learn another language? Learn survival skills?"

Why leave our singing in the shower?

My return to camp refreshed my memories of the *Why?* My fortnights in camp back then taught me to appreciate the counselors' knowledge, the benefits of the buddy system, and the value of the pack in a primitive setting. I can trace many of the principles of my life, especially appreciation for my fellow man, to my scouting experiences. I'm a lucky person to have had such an enriching opportunity.

Every year, in late July, just as the sun sets and the fireflies flash their lights for courtship, I reflect on the extraordinary times

I cherished at Scout Camp.

Showing her class, Coyote Woman embraced me. We rose from our bench and walked toward the setting sun as the crack of grasshoppers lifted from spent leaves, and the whip-poor-wills darted across the horizon.

Then I stopped and strained to hear another sound in the harmonics of the pines... It sounded like the camp bugler playing "Taps" was echoing through the trees.

. . . *Shadows of the evening lengthen, and day is done and peace at the last.*

"Do you hear that?"

She paused to look at me and listen. "I can hear the whining of the pines," she said.

"I thought I heard the familiar bugle call blown at night to signal lights out," I said, hearing "Taps" clearly now, "—sentimental old fool I am."

She smiled and sighed knowingly.

"Just the same," I whispered, "let's pause a moment longer, if you don't mind."

"Sure. Love you."

"I know."

HAY CREW
An Essay

"Hi, Ron! How you doin'?" George yelled as he raced across the field not unlike the record-setting trickster Roger Bannister. In one quick leap he was on the wagon and throwing bales with Pistol Pete.

The noise of the hay baler and tractor almost drowned out my response. "Hey, good to see you again, my Irish drinking buddy." Our hired hand, Pete, knew George only too well; they had tipped a few in town over the years. I was not surprised to hear them start singing the current hit by Bill Haley and His Comets, "Rock Around the Clock" as they had done frequently at our local tavern. No sooner had George and Pete started stacking bales on the wagon, I saw Dave—the limey—running down the lane from the barnyard.

"Hey! Good to see you, my English Prince. How've you been?" I yelled.

Without hesitation, our English blue blood climbed on the wagon and, sure enough, started singing his favorite, Frankie Laine's "High Noon." "Do not forsake me my darling…" Luckily the baling machine noise drowned out most of the singing—well, you get my point. I'll say this, it brought back memories of Gary Cooper walking down that lonely main street out west (I sure was annoyed at Grace Kelly's self-righteous attitude until she came to her senses and saved Gary with a Colt 45).

My dad Frank piloted his favorite 1943 John Deere B along the windrowed hay pulling the old 1950 I. H. (International Harvester) baler, knowing very well 'da boys had arrived. The noise of the chopping 'Chinaman' rising and falling, up and down, forward and back, which forced the hay into the individual battens forming a bale in the two foot square tunnel. I looked at Dad, and sure enough, that smirk on his face gave away the fact that he, too, could hear that singing—warts and all. (Okay, you'll have to ask the I. H. people why they call the vertical arm a 'Chinaman.')

To passersby and parked onlookers from the city, the three-pronged attack tractor (one person), baler (two people), and wagon (at least two) might appear to be moving at a glacial pace. At a distance, that may be true. But to the two on the baler's hand tying position, nothing could be further from the truth. Uncle Del and I had the job of hand-tying the wire bales as they pushed through the tunnel. It started with me plunging two 10-foot wires—with about 12-inch separation—into mechanical fingers that pulled the wires through the bale. The fingers would then push the wires back through the bale at about 8 battens, and I had to grab the loose ends. We wore leather gloves to protect our fingers from the sharp ends of the baling wire. Were Del and I glad when haying ended? You bet your life. But then again, it only lasted two or three days.

By the way, Del was a relative, not an uncle. But like so many of Dad and Mom's friends, I called them uncle or aunt because they acted as if they were. Quite frankly, 'the boys of summer haying' came close to being treated as cousins too. Why? They volunteered for the pleasure of helping Dad, and they'd do anything for him. That's family, right?

I think the boys' contact with Mom had a lot to do with their perfect timing. I can imagine her on the phone:

"Of course, come over; Frank will be baling Wednesday and Thursday. Is that a problem? No? Good. Thanks for offering. You'll pass the word? You're too kind. I'm anxious to see you boys again. I'll make sure you're well fed and Frank will certainly give your body a workout. Okay, dearie. See you later. Bye." (Of course, if it rains, Frank will have them fixing fence.)

No sooner had George and Dave started throwing bales with Pete on the wagon, another figure came running across the field, clearing each row as if a low-hurdling trickster. It was his old friend Milt.

"What's up, Ron?" Milt yelled over the baling noise. "Looks like you could use some help. I'm ready to rock and roll with some sweet-smelling hay. Where do we start?"

"Check with Dad," Ron replied. "I think he's ready to take a load to the barn. It's good to see you, you hurdler from the past."

Sure enough, Dad asked Milt to drive the Deere while he fetched another empty wagon with the Ford. Dad quickly unhitched the loaded wagon, attached the empty one, and told Milt to continue baling while he took the load to the barn.

"Keep your eyes on the boys while I'm gone, Pete!" Dad yelled as he headed to the barn.

On the way, Frank saw another young man from the past running across the field. Garvin threw not only bales, but also threw himself at Frank's niece Suzie.

"Jump on, Garvin," Frank said. "We'll get this load in the barn and return to the field before the next load is ready."

Garvin nodded and hopped on. "Good to see you, Frank," he said cheerfully.

With the aid of the huge elevator, they tucked away 80 bales into the corner of the barn, setting them next to the vent, allowing the hay to breathe. Back at the field, they discovered the entire gang was waiting; they had run out of baling wire.

After a quick look, Frank said, "No problem; we're losing daylight anyway. Let's leave everything in the field for tomorrow—we're not expecting rain tonight.

The whole gang jumped on the empty wagon and headed down the lane with Milt driving the Ford. And, you guessed it; they started singing Frankie Laine's "Mule Train"—in a six part harmony. Frank wore the look of a man worried the cattle may bolt as the voices reached the barnyard. He said later, he'd heard better croaking from frogs down by the river.

As in the past, before chow, all four volunteers—George, Dave, Milt, and Garvin—jumped in the stock tank to cool off and clean the hay chaff from their glistening bodies. Correction, George and Dave threw the reluctant Milt into the tank.

While drying off—and with a twinkle in his eye—George mentioned to Frank that a Budweiser would taste like right now. My proper English-born Mother chimed in, assuring the boys there wouldn't be any drinking of the suds while she was around.

"It's my homemade beer you'll be swilling," she said. "It'll be ginger ale and lemonade, so away with your blather."

They got the message—and a chuckle, too.

"Now get on over here, you rascals," Mom ordered, "your chicken pie and sweet corn await your pleasure. Come on now—and behave."

They all filed by Mom, each offering her a hug, as they used bales of hay as seating. A ten foot board set atop a pair of carpenter horses acted as a table; an elegant setting to these boys.

Marge spoke of her studies in American Indian folklore, comparing the evening meal to the Indian potlatch that honored those who served the tribe well. Frank passed a glance to Marge, signaling her to offer thanks to the Lord for nature's blessing.

Pete had set the traditional tub about fifty feet away so the boys could compete by pitching, tossing, and throwing corn cobs into it. It was hard telling who won because Fritz, my German shorthaired pointer, pranced and danced in front of the tub, catching and blocking shots like Cazzie Russell once did.

After each of the boys shared their favorite story of making hay and fixing fence on the farm, two things brought the evening to a close: George had to sing one of his favorites, which was Johnny Ray's "The Little White Cloud That Cried", and the sunset and dying fire finished the night. As the boys said goodbye to us, they gave Mom hugs and kisses on the cheek even as she was saying, "Away with all your blarney."

Milt wandered past the barn on his way to his truck, while asking if Frank could manage that last load without the others. "Yep," I assured him, answering for Dad. "But if you want to fix those downed fences…"

He wasn't having any of that. "I've got to take my dog to the vet," he said, climbing inside his truck.

Dad's lowered voice dispensed the truth of the matter. "He doesn't even own a dog," he said, headed out on his own.

I knew he wanted to be alone. There'd be a new baler delivered in the spring. Those sorts of machines had a way of taking jobs from men. But Pops, he'd surely find use for them elsewhere. There'd just be no need of tying those bales by hand.

*   *   *

We still baled hay every summer in early June for the first cutting, and late July for the second. Dad was right; the new baler needed just three of us rather than five with the old way. Later, with the addition of a roller baler, we'd only have use for a driver. That's quite a change from the days when Del and I would do the tying, Dad doing the driving, and two others on the wagon.

I'm not sure Del and I could accomplish those same tasks today, what with the arthritis of old age, and the fact those boys are all scattered across the country. A few still show up for that magic time each year, looking for real work to get the kinks out.

About five years later, Garvin stopped by with his new bride Suzie. While she and Mom chatted, Dad and I took Garvin out to the field to watch Pete on the new roller baler. Surprise stole across his face. The size of the machine was only the beginning of Garvin's shock. Even the old Ford had been modified to accommodate new technology. Counterweights and a hydraulically operated probe used for lifting the rolled bales further illustrated the lack of need for manual labor. Further talk moved to a newer, bigger baler just around the bend.

As we returned to the house and said our goodbyes, I heard Garvin chatting with Suzie, spilling all the news concerning innovations in baling. He'd had a great day just being with my folks on the farm. I, too, enjoyed the fellowship associated with the gang at haying time in those early 1950s. That is all shuttered now, though the memories linger. These experiences can never be taken from us; they should be embraced and shared with our children. At times we seem to want to airbrush certain aspects of our lives—like hand-tying bales of hay. But good or bad, we generally learn from these experiences.

I'm a fortunate guy with my bride of four years now. My parents have their health Mom still makes her pot roast every Sunday. Pete, well, he'll always be a bachelor. The boys of summer always remember Mom and Dad with a card at Christmas. Not just any old card, either. There's usually a farm scene, a John Deere, a baler, or a harvest table surrounded by friends.

*   *   *

I have taken the liberty to combine several of my experiences with many fine young men while working on the farms of Frank Redick, Samuel Parker, and Ivan Galpin, from 1950 to 1960.

A CHRISTMAS SURPRISE

An Essay

The circled campers watched the sun slide into the lake with the same pulsing reddish-orange glow that radiated from the campfire. The nameless assemblage were sharing end-of summer stories on the beach as autumn's beauty faded to winter's disrobed landscape.

From the throng, an unrevealed Native American's gentle voice spoke of similar fall storms in his past that transformed the beach from gusting sand to swirling snow as children waited anxiously for the holiday season excitement.

*   *   *

The gentle-hearted native spoke of the world as unpretentious in the mid-forties, when the Christmas holiday embraces the families within the tribes of Northern Michigan. Most had little income for gifts—especially for children of tribal families along the

Lake Michigan shoreline. Their spiritual beliefs were a blend of Native, Christian, and contemporary myths—including Santa Clause. Local merchandising did not escape the attentions of children on the reservation; Santa and the spirit of Christmas influenced everything.

Even at the young age of four everyone called him Little Chief, and like other kids, he anticipated the arrival of Christmas—even without decorations, a yule tree, or gifts inside their modest home. Yet, his stocking hung by the potbelly stove where Santa would surely find it. And even though nobody had mentioned gifts or a special Christmas meal, his head had filled with wonder and excitement. By the night before Christmas, there remained little time to prepare.

Sadly, his mother lay in bed with an illness he could not understand. She'd not been herself. She had begun to gain weight. Nevertheless, she could still laugh and joke with his father about things the young boy could not comprehend—even as a preoccupied mind had captured his father's thoughts. But how could there be problems on Christmas Eve?

His expression animated, he spoke of his father, hands cupped to his ears, saying, "What's that noise? Sounds like sleigh bells to me." Then he added, "Sshhh…listen." He went to the window. "Yup," he exclaimed. "There he goes."

Anticipation yanked him to the window. Expectations ran high. Surely he'd glimpse Santa gliding through the cold moonlit night. But there was no Santa to be seen. Disappointment had settled in. Santa had certainly forgotten him. "My son," his father explained, "do not be sad. Santa did not stop because you were not in bed. I'm sure if you go to bed Santa will come back and bring you a real special present." With eyes gleaming and his heart beating fast, the boy bolted up the stairs and into bed. A winter chill filled the room—so much so that he could see his breath. With the colorful patchwork quilt pulled over his head, his thoughts began to roam. Behind his closed eyes, notions of what Santa might bring burned brightly in the night. His fingers took hold on the amulet at his neck. Above his head, that Dream Catcher would filter only the best wishes for him. Sleep came quickly as a howling wind whistled its eerie song over the barren shoreline landscape.

*   *   *

Shards of sunlight pulled the boy from his sleep—as did the smell of bacon and fried potatoes. For a moment the scent of his favorite breakfast stole all his thoughts. But this was Christmas morning. The idea that Santa had left a gift chased him from his bed. Down the stairs he went. He pushed open the door at the bottom. A rush of warm air welcomed the boy into the room. His eyes searched for that gift Santa surely left behind.

His gaze wandered the room. An old rounded steamer trunk rested beside his mother's bed. Her eyes met his. A shared smile passed between them. His mother looked well, healthy. Santa had indeed returned to their humble home. He'd left a special present in the trunk. The boy ran to the trunk. He balanced himself on his tiptoes, gripped the trunk with his little hands, and had a peek at the gift Santa brought especially for him.

Amazement and joy filled his heart and head. He had a new baby brother. But who should he thank: his parents or Santa?

"Do you want to hold him?" his mother asked.

Of course he wanted to hold him. He climbed on the bed and nestled against his mother. His father gathered the newest member of the family and placed the baby across big brother's arms.

"His name is Little Beaver," his father said. "Be a good big brother to him and help him through life's challenges."

"Can I play with him now?" the boy asked. "Can I pull him on my sled?" Never before had he felt this much pride and joy.

His mother smiled and said, "Of course you can—but you'll

have to wait a while. It's been big day and a very Merry Christmas. Don't you think we've been blessed?"

The boy answered, "We sure have been blessed. The Great Spirit must have heard my prayers. I can't wait to go fishing with Little Beaver."

*　　*　　*

The humble Native paused, lit his pipe, and continued as to why he shared his Christmas Surprise with us. He and his father had a fire on the beach that night similar to the one here, he explained. They thanked the Creator for mother and baby's health and the blessed event.

He rose and thanked us for sharing our fire. He walked down the beach in what I suppose was a moment to reflect on the past in his own chosen solitude.

*　　*　　*

As we reflect on the Indian's splendid story around the campfire, shouldn't the lesson for all of us be to hold fast to the memories of those experiences we've shared with our parents, family, and friends? We never know what each day will bring—unimagined joy or the unknown. Even when we fear the worst sometimes we find ourselves celebrating the best.

Why not light a fire on the beach tonight—or, for that matter, light one anywhere. Go ahead, give it a try; you just might experience a blessed event.

A FAMILY TREE

An Essay

The majestic spruce stood out from the oaks and maples, high-lighted on a slope, surrounded by a patch of tall grass that faded into the woods. From the crest of the hill looked over a pastoral sea toward the farm. The worn path was barely discernable under a fresh blanket of snow. Her verdant boughs glistened in the moonlight while shadows danced across the sparkling surface.

Across the meadow she observed the children of her adoptive family rollicking in the snow. Her family? Yes, her dense lower branches presented a hideout, a windbreak, war council rendez-vous, and many other childhood activities. She longed for their presence. But, as with seasonal change, they now played close to the farmyard. The robin, too, had departed with her chicks, but in leaving, surely had planned to return to her nest now held in the safety of the spruce's boughs. As she watched the children playing she sensed the cheer of the holidays in their hearts, and shifting their activities away from her during this time, she would be alone.

Regardless of her lonely thoughts, she stood tall in her new shroud of shimmering snow. She was and had always been Queen of the meadow—outlanders noticed her presence.

*   *   *

Her reflection of summer's joy transformed as a pair with bounding flashlights crossed the meadow from an unusual direction. She did not recognize these two, but understood the meaning of the handsaw and coil of rope they'd brought along. *Am I about to be harvested?* She shuddered at the thought. *Will I lose my life to this holiday?* As the men approached, a squirrel chattered a protest against such an intrusion before scampering up a neighboring oak.

"This one will do," one of the men announced. "It's the perfect size and shape for the lobby."

Her boughs drooped in sad preparation on her fate as a Christmas tree.

They raised her lower boughs to gain access to her trunk.

Then a noise across the meadow startled the pair…

With flashlights in hand, a group approached from the house. A quick assessment of the situation sent the two strangers on their way to try finding better success at the local tree farm.

Children and parents alike went to work around the tree.

"Is the extension cord long enough?"

"Yep, I'm almost to the top."

"Hit the switch. Let's see how she looks."

"Beautiful!" the leader proclaimed. "You've never looked so radiant, my dear. Merry Christmas."

*   *   *

You know what happened. The family had crowned the

spruce with a lighted star so it too could be part of the holiday celebration...part of the family.

Each of us can play a similar part during the holidays by sharing a little light with those in need of the shine from your heart.

CALL ME MARGE

An Essay

Another winter storm covers the earth as the tractor plods its way through the whitening field of corn. In the distance bare trees are delicate pencil strokes against the luminous whiteness. The crisp November day embraced our farm and my body while our old reliable John Deere navigated through the corn rows. Sometimes called Jumping Johnny, the old two-cylinder Deere barked in a melodic rhythm. That sound, that feel, that experience of picking corn in the cool crisp air was like winning a Grand Slam. I loved farming Mother Nature's breast.

Another reason for my love of farming was the figure unexpectedly standing by the fence line hailing me.

There she was, my classic English mom, with her British traits still intact forty years after leaving England in 1920. Five feet five, ramrod straight, with a fading English accent, and phrases embedded in her DNA:

"Be careful or you'll muck it up."

"That will be enough; away with you."

"Go away with your mither."

There she stood in her trademark babushka, long coat, and huge hand made scarf wrapped around her neck. Here's the gal from a fairly wealthy home who came over in her preteen years, married Dad in 1929 and lived in a beautiful home in Downriver Detroit for 21 years, and in a major life-changing decision, moved to the farm—for Dad—in 1950. The shock of scratching out a living did not seem to bother her. Then Dad died in 1955.

There she is, not complaining, and most importantly, not giving up on Dad's dream of returning to the farm. Over those tough years, at 50 now, she had silently, without expressing dissatisfaction, experienced every tilt imaginable. One anecdotal story demonstrates her true grit: After Dad died, when Mom was at the mill one day in her old reliable '46 Dodge PU, Ron, the owner, referred to her in some fashion using the term "widow." To wit, she immediately corrected him, saying, "Call me Marge." Unsaid was the fact that she was now on her own and did not need a reminder of her past. Those days were over.

*   *   *

There she was trotting out while I shut down the corn picker and idled the Deere. I ask myself, "How does she go on?" She never complained, never cried in front of us boys—though she did cry at night.

As she walked over to the rig, I bounded off the tractor. I thought to myself, this must be important.

"Sorry to bother you," she said, "but I need your help."

"No problem," I replied. "What's up?"

She explained that she had run the numbers and we'd need $100 to get through the month. Could I take two loads of corn to the mill that day?

I assured her I could. There were already two loads on that wagon.

"Go to Joe's mill in Milan, or to Sparrow's in Willis," she said.

I chose Joe's. Joe always did us right.

Over the noise of the engagement of the PTO to the corn picker, I yelled to Mom to throw a lunch together to eat while at the mill.

"And get me a couple of sacks of paisley print feed supplement," she ordered before turning toward home. "Make sure it's paisley—not floral. You'll be wearing it for PJs and a shirt."

*   *   *

There's more stories about Marge, but this reflection says it all: she was a survivor. We made a go of it for five years and sold the farm since all of us had to move on with our lives. We graduated, moved out of state, married, and joined the military.

In later years, with pride and pleasure, we share some of those memories of those years. Our children really enjoy looking at— and wearing for fun—the pajamas made for us in the early 1950s. That distinctive label reads: Creations by Marge.

BIG JIM
An Essay

My days in the '50s as a sixteen-year-old working at a farm for my dad's friend Ivan proved rather enriching—and sometimes troublesome.

"You do not have to do this," I pleaded with Ivan on that day everything seemed to go wrong. "Jim meant no harm. He was just protecting his herd, his harem, your breeding stock; and I was challenging his supremacy."

"Nice try," Ivan pronounced, his face stern, arms crossed resolutely, "but my decision is final. It's no longer safe to keep a breeding bull like Jim with the herd. He'll stop at nothing to defend his domain. He's served his and my needs for three years very well, but as expected he's becoming more *bullish* with age."

Pistol Pete backed the stock carrier up to the loading chute. He jumped down from his truck, spit tobacco juice at a scurrying bug, and shifted a wad of chew to the other side of his jaw. "Got him!" pronounced Pete, sounding a lot like Dirty Harry as he eyed the bug wallowing in spit.

I'd been wanting to ask Pete how he got the nickname, but I was too frustrated with Ivan right then.

"Let's get him loaded," Pete ordered, now sounding like John Wayne in *True Grit.* "Daylight is burning!" In constant motion, he wiped his hands on soiled Levis, tipped back his John Deere cap to scratch his head, then kicked the dirt with his worn-down boots. "Do I have to get him me-self while you two argue till the cows come home? Once or twice a week I pick up one of these toros that up and decided to treat his owner like a matador."

I didn't appreciate his characterization of Jim's one-time isolated, um, *incident.*

"Hold your horses," Ivan said, screwing his face up and scratching his frazzled beard. "I'd send the boy to get him, but the way he's all choked up I'm afraid he'd turn him a-loose."

I started to protest, but Ivan grabbed the bull pole and headed for the barn. He came out leading Jim by the pole hooked through his nose ring. He deftly moved the massive beast into the stock truck without incident.

Closing the loading chute, Pete hollered, "Was *that* the dangerous bull you called me out here to get? He looks like a big one-ton baby to me."

He was right about that; Jim had never been a problem before that fateful day.

Ivan looked away without saying anything. I reached through the stock rack to scratch behind Jim's ears, just as I'd done so many times in his box stall. If only Jim could talk... The look in his eyes said he knew his fate. He'd seen the truck many times when older cattle that no longer produced enough milk rode off, never to be seen again.

"Jim," I said to the bull quietly, hoping Pete and Ivan wouldn't hear. They were jawing about the cost of running a farm. "Jim, this is a mistake. You're not dangerous."

What a waste.

Ivan would have to get another bull anyway, and Jim wouldn't bring in much per pound, him being a bologna bull—tough meat, no prime cuts. It just didn't make sense. Jim had at least two more years left in him as the herd sire.

Worse, Jim's imminent demise was all my fault.

*   *   *

"Come on, Sandy! Let's go!" I called on a routine evening two days before. Two-year-old collie/Labrador mix Sandy and I were late bringing the herd in for milking. "Good girl! I couldn't do this without your help."

Sandy had proved herself time and again to be the perfect partner for herding the cattle from pasture to the barn's milking parlor. The cattle feared her more than they feared me; I didn't nip at their hind legs to get them moving in the right direction. She'd even clamp onto a tail every now and then when a cow's stubbornness required it. Yes, Sandy had been kicked a few times, but she seemed to accept that it came with the job.

I always loved the times Sandy and I walked down the lane. I talked to her and, yes, she acknowledged my comments, concerns, complaints, and adolescent feelings about life. She listened to the frustrations of my burgeoning romantic encounters, which ebbed and flowed—most leaving flotsam on the shore. Sandy would wait for me to finish, then stop, look at me, cock her head, and whine. I was always sure that meant she agreed with my laments. I wanted to ask her, "What would *you* do?" but I knew empathy was the best she could muster.

As we left the lane and entered the back forty, Sandy gave me that *Can I take off?* look. She whined as I called out greeting to the neighbor baling hay in his field next to Ivan's pasture.

"Sorry, girl." I gave her the nod, and before I could say, "Okay, babe," she was off and running through the sun-drenched, richly verdant grass, fast as her legs could carry her. Her gracefulness was a thing of beauty, but her intensity impressed the most. She was on a mission.

As I walked toward the cattle at the bottom of the pasture, she raced after the forty or so Holsteins. About twenty were milkcows, the rest heifers and calves . . .

And of course, Big Jim.

Jim's job was rather simple: whenever a cow or heifer was in heat, he took care of business. Forty head kept him busy year-round. At times, he'd let you know it was *his* herd—don't mess with the monarch—but he had always behaved like a gentle giant.

I walked around the massive old oak tree we called Big Ben. Ivan named everything on the farm—plant, animal, mineral, sometimes including the *Big* when appropriate. I headed toward the fence line to check for breaches and stumbled upon a pair of fraternal calves in the tall grass.

Looking back at what happened next, it makes sense. Newborns have survival instincts hard-wired into their brains by eons of evolutionary pressure, likely all the way back to life on the African Serengeti. That day, as I walked toward the calves, the bull calf leaped up, lowered his head, and charged into my leg—again and again. Then just as quickly, he tired and lay down again with his twin.

Still, while I was busy admiring the bull-calf's visceral display, I failed to notice Big Jim heading my way.

He seemed to be in a hurry.

Sandy was nipping at his tail, but that didn't distract him from his mission one bit. As I looked up, she started jumping at his flanks and barking to distract him, maybe giving him a chance to calm down.

Undeterred, Big Jim was coming for me!

With no way out, I headed for Big Ben.

I hid behind the trunk, but Jim wasn't fooled.

He charged around the tree and thrust at me with his muscular shoulder, thick neck, and sharp horns.

I kept moving around the tree, trying to keep him on the other side, but he danced with amazing nimbleness, parrying and thrusting. I'd thought it funny the way the little bull was charging did.

*   *   *

But Big Jim was no joke.

Sandy kept the pressure on him, past trying to calm him, now just trying to scare him away. She lunged repeatedly between Jim and me, protecting me with her life.

Over time farmers had thrown stones at the tree, so when Jim made a couple of bad steps on rocks, he got frustrated, then hesitant. He glared at me, then snorted, bellowed, pawed the ground, and hurried off to rejoin his herd.

"Good girl," I told Sandy, adding a respectful thanks to the regal old Big Ben. She hurried off to finish gathering the herd and start moving them toward the barn.

As they passed by me, Jim ambled along, his usual docile self, watching over his ladies. Then he glanced my way, looking somehow sheepish, maybe even embarrassed. Breeding hormones had kicked up his base instincts, and now he felt bad about threatening an old friend.

"Hey, Jim! It's okay," I yelled at him.

I thought that would be the end of it. I certainly didn't intend the tell Ivan what happened.

But the neighbor bailing hay did.

*   *   *

As he climbed into the cab, Pete let out a yell: "Big Jim'll be baloney by this time tomorrow! See ya!"

As Pete pulled out, I could see Jim looking at us one last time. He knew.

Sigh.

I'd considered what happened to be an isolated event, but Ivan made a good point: once a bull lets his instinct take over, he becomes a danger to the people on the farm. What if Big Ben hadn't been there to shield me? What if Sandy had been gored? What if Ivan's daughter had been with me?

Ivan was right. It had to be done.

A bull has his time, and while it lasts it is a great life. I mean, who can argue with long days taking it easy, his only responsibility keeping his harem of the prettiest gals serviced?

"Let's go to the stock auction tomorrow," Ivan said as we walked back toward the barn, "—need to get us a bull."

That's right, life goes on, and a whole herd of pretty gals awaited the next lucky fella.

"You've gotten durn good," Ivan added, "at recognizing good stock." I did appreciate the acknowledgement, a chance for my sixteen-year-old self to feel good about what I'd learned working with the older man. "You," he pronounced, "can select our next bull."

That got me to smile.

I did find us a good bull, but somehow none seemed like he could ever replace Big Jim.

BUGLE BOY

Historical Family-based Fiction

The major theme of "Bugle Boy" is to tell the story of the deep relationship that develops between Andrew, the bugle boy, and his
grandfather Wesley in the setting of the Civil War 1861 to 1865.

It is a historically accurate account of the Union Army's 75th
Ohio Volunteer Infantry (OVI) as they battled the Confederates
in the Civil War at Gettysburg in July of 1863—the turning
point of the war for the Union.

The key characters are Wesley Redick, my great paternal
grandfather; his cousin Captain William Redick; Frank De-
Sellum, armorer; Sergeant Wilson, the chief communicator; and
Wesley's 14-year-old grandson, Andrew Redick. Andrew is the

*company's bugler/ messenger. Wesley's portrayals are factually ac-
curate, Andrew's fictional.*

*The story describes a brief portion of the successes and failures
of battles between Union and Confederate troops, those in command, and how the typically horrific loss of life affects them.*

*   *   *

The battlefield smoke billowed along the ridge line to the east.
The caustic cloud-like presence partially masked the morning sun.
A slight breeze slowly moved the mask, shielding the battle's car-
nage to the ridge line on the horizon. Andrew, the bugle boy, was
frightened. He was not certain he wanted to see the fighting. He
could imagine the terror his ears could hear, but his eyes could
not see. He was alone, save for the various wagons and horses
and a few foot soldiers on sentry duty. Terror-stricken of the unknown, he felt as if his bones rattled. He was concerned. Andrew
feared for the safety of his granddad. This was the first experience
in support of Union troops, for his "Gramps," too. Fighting the
Confederates was a new threat for everyone. He was scared.

Andrew was waiting for his next order. Earlier, he had been
told to sound "Assembly" . . . then: "Boots and Saddles" . . . and
finally: "Charge" as the combined infantry and cavalry of the
Ohio 75th joined the brigade to their left and right flanks, and
charged over the ridge. As the bugle's sound echoed over the hillock, a rush of pride filled his chest. The infantry advanced while
taking a final check of their weapons . . . the cavalry steadied their
spirited mounts as the major shouted orders . . . their swords
thrust in the air.

Following his orders, Andrew returned to the headquarters
area and stood by the tent, waiting for further instructions. He
knew better than ask the major for permission to join the charge;
it was clear that he was not about to take any unnecessary chances
with Andrew's life.

This was the first encounter by the 75th as it moved into its attack formation to effectively roust the Confederate troops dug in.

Andrew remembered Wesley's stern command very well. "Go!" he shouted. "Do not stop until you reach the company area . . .   Go!"

Andrew ran to the rear as fast as his legs would carry him. He heard the cannon's canister rounds of grape-shot riddle the trees overhead. A "Minie ball" struck a limb to his left, shattering it to bits . . .   he ran faster. He shivered in fear knowing what the company faced along the frontal assault. After several minutes running, he hit-the-deck after arriving at the HQ's tent . . .   he shook as much as the cannon's report jarred the earth. He asked God to protect the men.

*   *   *

On the village green in Logan, Ohio

Lincoln's first call for troops in May, 1861, stirred interest in the men of Columbiana County, Ohio. Many of the local farmers answered the call posted on the courthouse bulletin board. The posting was direct and to the point:

Volunteers needed to form the
75th Ohio Volunteer Infantry OVI.
Those interested should come to the
courthouse this Saturday.
Signed: Wesley Redick

*   *   *

The War Between Brothers

Wes felt as though by talking to the troops he had purged many of the problems that had plagued his decisions as a commander. He had never been in a position like this before. Now his decisions, right or wrong, good or bad, cost lives. It was true, the men had volunteered to serve in the 75th. For many and varied reasons they had chosen war. Many of the single men were simply adventurous with an aggressive, combative personality; others, those married, exhibited a more cautious style. A common trait was their desire to fight Johnny Reb and his defiant attitude, his disregard for the Union, and his "radical" Southern crusade for secession. Both types of Union fighters were targets for the Rebel "ball" regardless of their reasons for fighting. Once armed, Rebel sharpshooters targeted the *uniform*, the enemy . . . whether friend, foe, or yes, even a relative. The operative word from commanders was "kill or be killed" and "do not hesitate even if your neighbor is in your sights. This is true, especially when his rifle is aimed at you."

Wes had noticed Andrew's melancholy mood as the campaign wore on and the trauma of death and destruction faced him daily. He quickly found Andrew with DeSellum and joined them by his pinto, Chico.

"How you doin', son? Is your favorite steed holding up as we prance around the hills and valleys of Virginia? He is certainly a beautiful horse. How old is he?" asked Wes.

"Oh, hi, Gramps. He's about eight years old . . . going on twelve with this campaign of the 75th. Frank was just showing me how to clean his hoof frog with a tool he made. It's slick for digging out stones and small pieces of shrapnel."

"I thought he was going lame or something."

"No, just needed some maintenance. Frank also showed me how to trim his hooves and give him new shoes. The blacksmith let us use his tools and forge this morning."

"Sounds good to me, can I take a look?"

"Help yourself."

Wes lifted up each of Chico's legs individually and examined how well Andrew had shod his horse.

"Hey, good job, I'll know where to come when *my* horse needs some shoes," Wes said while Wes patted Chico's flanks and chatted about horses.

Frank seemed to sense their need to be alone.

"See you in the morning, Andrew. Keep up the good work. I'll be waiting for your melodic 'Taps.' See, ya."

While leaving, Frank checked all the horses on the picket line where they were tethered, and left the two by themselves.

Wes asked if Andrew would like to have a snack in his headquarters tent. The boy would know, without a doubt, that it would be his grandfather's favorite ginger-snap cookies. The answer was an eager, "Yes." They walked shoulder to shoulder across the encampment in the early evening twilight. On the way, Wes asked him to sit on a log by a vacated camp firepit.

Wes spoke. "You've carried yourself very well in the Company, son. I'm proud of your performance in the face of adversity. War is hell, isn't it? Although we've taken our licks from Johnny Reb, his luck has just about run out. They're on the move again, and we'll be following them as they move north. To where, I've no idea . . . maybe Washington, for all I know. I'll be giving the marching orders in the morning. One way or the other, we will stop them from reaching Washington. We'll be on their eastern flank every step of the way. One of us will decide when to fight . . . and I guarantee you, if they head east to our capital, we will engage. It will be a donnybrook, a brawl, a free-for-all. This may be Lee's last chance to launch a major offensive. His troop strength has weakened considerably this year. Yes, he's won several fights, but lost many brigades doing so.

"I suppose you wonder what I'm leading up to? Here's my point: Encounters will be more dangerous now. They will be overwhelming. Son, Lee is desperate. There will be unreasonable demands put on his troops to attack at all costs. As such, I'm concerned for your safety.

"As a family, we have lost William, and I do not want to lose you. Do you see where I'm going with this?"

"No," said Andrew, his voice wary.

"I want you to leave the 75th and serve in the rear with Corps Headquarters. You'll still be supporting our unit, our brigade, our president, our country. There's no need for you to stay in harm's way during these last few skirmishes. I'm thinking of your future, your mom's concerns, and yes . . . mine. Do you understand my feelings?"

"Yes . . . yes, but you can save your breath. I'm even more resolved to stay since Uncle Bill's death, and to pay homage to my fellow men of the 75th. If necessary, I choose to fight 'til death for our noble cause.

"No, Gramps, I'm staying 'til the bitter end. My emotions are certainly tied to the country and the president, but they are more permanently tied to your unit—my unit—the 75th. These men are who I fight with and care for. I couldn't let them down; they depend on me, too. Oh, it may be in minor ways, but nevertheless, I'm there when they need something. Only a Rebel round will end my support for my fellow Union soldiers while the men of the 75th are still fighting."

Silence.

Wes hugged Andrew around the waist as they walked to the tent for cookies. Andrew's emotions were clear. Wes did not challenge them. He was a proud grandfather . . . Indeed, very proud.

They had a good night dunking cookies in coffee and milk until Andrew had to leave to blow "Taps."

Wes had been favored by taps many times over the years, but

tonight's sound seemed clearer, stronger, and of a more whole-some tone than he had ever heard before.

Wes thought, as Andrew turned in for the night, *Rest well, young man. May God be with you over the next few months.*

*   *   *

As Wes had predicted, in June 1863, Lee's army swung up the Shenandoah Valley into Pennsylvania. Both armies moved to-ward the little town of Gettysburg. The shooting started when a Confederate brigade, searching for shoes in town, ran into Union cavalry on July 1. This incident triggered one of the most decisive battles of the Civil War. Southern troops at 65,000 strength fought the Northern army of 85,000 during this fateful three-day period in our history.

On the first day, Northern troops were pushed east and south of town and later driven up a slope to the south. They finally set-tled in a defensive location resembling a fishhook, the curved "hook" to the north, and the rest of the men strung in a southerly line. With the hook at Culp's hill and the troops along Cemetery Hill, it made for a very strong defensive line that terminated to the south at Little Round Top.

Confederate forces occupied Gettysburg to the north, and Seminary Ridge to the west.

On July 2, the second day of fighting, Lee tried a flanking at-tack up Cemetery Hill toward Little Round Top. Lee's first assault crushed the first line of defense. However, on the top of the hill where the 75th dug in, the Northern lines held. In an extended, vicious battle, countless times the Rebels attacked up the hill only to be thwarted by the continuous rattle of musketry and withering cannon fire by a superior Union line of defense. Many men fought bravely to save the day, both at Little Round Top and Culp's hill on the opposite flank.

*   *   *

During the attack on Cemetery Hill, desperate to hold the line and running low on ammunition, Wes asked Frank to go back to the Company area for more ammo.

"Frank! Frank, over here."

Ka-Boom! A canister round exploded overhead.

"Frank! Do you hear me?"

Ka-Pow. A round almost took Wes's head off as he raised up to see Frank. "Yep, I'm over here," he answered over the roar of bursting shells. "Over here. I need to see you."

"Okay, I'll see if I can crawl over between bursts," Frank yelled as he moved toward Wes. Musket rounds fell to his left, to his right, and they whizzed overhead as he crawled over dead and dying men in his path. Those who could speak cried out for help as he slithered by.

"There you are. You okay?"

"Yep, I guess. The blood you see all over my clothes is not mine. I had to crawl over many dead and wounded. What do you need?"

"Ammo! We need *much* more ammo. We're running out. Jones, who normally would make the run, is wounded and unable to go. Can you go for us?"

"Sure, just keep an eye on my men. I won't be gone that long."

He crawled away about 30 feet, looked ahead to the right and left, stood up to run . . . and—

Ka-Pow!

Frank went down like a sack of flour and rolled over, grabbing his leg.

"Frank! Frank! Are you okay?" Wes yelled.

He yelled, "Let me check . . . yeah . . . I think I'll be okay . . . it's just a flesh wound . . . yeah, I'll just hold my leg tight and it will probably stop bleeding. Damn, isn't that something? I almost got shot in the arse. Now that would be hard to explain to my men."

Ka-Boom! Another canister round exploded overhead.

"Okay, you rascal, get going and be sure to see the medics as soon as you return. We'll try to hold off these screamin' Rebs until you get back."

Frank got up again while holding his leg, and ran to the rear not unlike a chimp's loping sway. So as to be unencumbered by his rifle, be took Wes's pistol for protection.

*   *   *

Assuming that Private Jones would be coming for more ammo, Andrew had already loaded several haversacks with .58 ball and percussion caps. He was also helping the wounded to the brigade medical tent nearby.

Clearing a hillock to the front, Frank arrived in a slow, staggering crouch. It appeared that he was hurting pretty badly.

"Frank! Are you okay?" Andrew yelled.

"Yep. Ammo, Andy, we need ammo up front . . . we're about to run out. Jones is hurt, so I'm taking the run for him. I took a round in the leg . . . I'm losing blood faster than I thought . . . get some ammo . . . quickly," he moaned.

"Okay, Frank." He turned and picked up several haversacks and brought them to Frank.

He threw them over Frank's neck and shoulders—and he collapsed. "Frank, you're in no condition to go back. Here, have a drink from my canteen."

"Thanks. I'll be okay. I just need to rest a little."

Through fatigue, blood loss, and increasing pain, Frank's wound had taken its toll. He asked for another drink, then rinsed his wound with a little water. When Andrew saw the torn muscle and bloody mass under his pant leg, he decided he had to take over Frank's task. Frank wasn't going back; he was going to the medical tent.

"I say again, Frank, you're in no condition to go back. I'll make the run for you. I'm going to carry you over to the medical tent right now, and then I'll take the ammo to the men."

"Okay, you're right. But go now . . . forget about me . . . I'll crawl to the medics . . . and be aware, I'll be in trouble with Wes for letting you go to the front."

"Not to worry, I'm the only healthy one here. Besides, I'm in charge now. I'm taking you first," Andrew said as he took the haversacks from around Frank's neck, lifted him up, and threw him over his shoulder.

Frank yelled, "No . . . get going . . . no . . . don't!" and he passed out, either due to shock, fatigue, or both.

Andrew now spoke to him as if the company's sergeant. "Frank, I suppose you'll tell me that I'm disobeying a direct order, and you'll take one of my stripes . . . But, I've got news for you . . . I have no stripes . . . ha . . . now, be quiet."

After dropping him off, Andrew picked up Frank's pistol and haversacks of ammo, and ran toward the front.

*   *   *

Ka-Boom!

Wes kept looking to the rear for Frank. After a short lull, the Rebs were about to try advancing again. As expected, the sound of steady footfalls of a column, the tinkling noise made by bayonets striking tin cups, and the clanking and clanging of arms carried up the slope indicating the Rebs were about to attack. Seminary Ridge was about to explode.

The 75th waited. The new sound—silence—on the battlefield was deafening.

The time for attack was at hand; the men of Wes's company tended to final rituals. Friends sought out friends and wished each other well until after the battle. Wes had directed all officers dismounted as they passed along the lines attending to the needs of their men. Many in the company had scribbled a letter to their loved ones and announced, "Sir, I feel this is the last letter I will write." Reluctantly, Wes accepted the letters.

Now Wes reminded his men to "Remember what Ohio and our friends at home expect of us."

Fearing the possibilities of being overrun for lack of ammo, Wes passed on an unfortunate, but practical, command down the line. "Fix bayonets."

Wes was reminded of his recent training that surprisingly resolved that Civil War tactics were still fashioned after Napoleon Bonaparte's Armies (early 1800s). Frequently commanders accepted the practice of using the bayonet as a last resort. But by 1862, after First Manassas (Bull Run), the rifle musket now in use on both sides had rendered the bayonet charge foolish. While Napoleon's charging lines at Waterloo had been exposed to musket fire for a hundred yards, the rifle muskets could destroy a charging line with accuracy from 350 yards, and do damage at more than 500 yards.

By 1862, battle lines infrequently were close enough to engage in a classic hand-to-hand fight. In this case, Wes needed the bayonet for defensive purposes. If he ran out of ammo, the bayonet's cold steel blade may be his last line of defense . . . the crucial element between life and death.

Wes paused and gave a more encouraging order. "Select your targets carefully, boys . . . with limited ammo, drop those Rebs like the wind does the leaves in autumn."

To strengthen the Union cannon batteries, Wes helped an artillery sergeant unlimber their cannon and move the horses, with flanks and muzzles covered with foam and eyes ablaze with fear, team to the rear. While helping the team move their gun into position, he thought, *Where is Frank? I hope that bullet didn't have his final number on it. Wait a minute . . . what's that?*

With his eyes straining to see through the battleground smoke, Wes saw a figure running toward him. It wasn't Frank . . . he rose slightly to get a better view. He was shocked at what he saw . . . it looked like Andrew. He was running in a zig-zag pattern as all infantry men were taught. Being in a crouch, or bent-over stance, he wasn't sure . . . until the figure got closer and Wes was sure who it was.

Wes yelled, "Get down, Andrew, the Rebs are about to attack. Crawl! For heaven's sake . . . get down on your belly. This whole area's going to be filled with 'Minie balls' at any moment."

"No, Gramps, can't yet . . . Frank says I've got to give out this ammo up and down the line . . . I'll be back in a second . . . Oh, here's yours."

He threw a sack toward Wes, and crawled along the line giving the remaining sacks to the four platoons.

Ka-Pow! Ka-Pow!

As Andrew leaped over, around, and through the detritus of logs, rock, and bodies . . . some wounded, others dead, he finally made it back to Wes.

"Yip—Yip—A-A-E-E-EEEEEE," suddenly rose from the attacking Johnny Rebs; the yelping screams shattered the air and echoed across the Union Lines.

"Get down, Andy, here they come . . . hit the dirt."

Andy leaped behind the Union fortifications in front of Wes, gave him another sack, caught his breath, and quickly started loading a rifle musket like the others on the line.

While shooting and reloading, Wes yelled over the battle sounds, "Son, no matter what, don't expose yourself to enemy fire like that again . . . we don't need any more fearless fighters falling . . . now get out of here—get!"

"Okay, Gramps. I was just filling in for Frank."

"I know . . . and you did it well, but you're too young to be up here. I promised your mother I wouldn't put you in harm's way . . . whenever possible. By the way, how is Frank?"

"He'll make it, but a 'Minie ball' rearranged his quad muscle. I took him to the brigade medical unit."

Ka-Boom! Iron pellets showered the area from a canister charge. *Ka-Pow! Ka-Pow! Ka-Pow! Ziiinnnggg! Ka-Boom!* Echoed across the front as the charge began.

Wes repeated, "Fine, now get . . . one thing, did Frank ask you to bring this ammo?"

"No. He had passed out by then."

"Figures. Now get!" said Wes as he turned to face the charging Rebs.

*   *   *

While running back, a series of cannon bursts along his return route made Andrew alter his course back to the 75th. He circled around the southeast side of Little Round Top and headed northeast to reach Company Headquarters. He held his position a moment and looked around for a landmark or two to ensure he was on the right course.

He thought, *Ah, this is the way, I'll head for that toppled pine to the northeast . . . yeah, that'll work.*

He caught his breath, took a short swig from his canteen, checked his pistol, then took a long draft . . . and paused.

As he stepped off, a noise by a downed pine tree caught his attention. He paused. "What's that?"

He looked around the area for the source of the sound. It was very weak sounding, like a moan. "O-O-HH-aa." A mournful cry.

"There it is again."

Andrew thought, *I'd better check; it could be one of our wounded.*

With his half-cocked .45 Colt leading the way, he walked toward the sound. He carefully stepped over the boulders and trees downed by cannon fire . . .

Ka-Boom!

He hit the deck.

With the aid of the flashing burst overhead, just ahead . . . a supine body with a pained face stared back at Andrew.

For a moment, in the dynamics of the fierce battleground, he turned to stone.

"I'll be darned," Andrew cried as his eyes caught the eyes of the injured man. Pressed in a soiled gray uniform, it appeared to be a Johnny Reb. The soldier's rifle lay near his feet, an empty canteen by his side, and a red-to-black stain on his upper right arm indicated a serious wound. Additionally, most of the sleeve was torn away with a blood wrap encircling his upper arm.

With a strong Southern drawl, he said, "No—no—don't shoot—leave me alone . . . I want to die, I'm bleeding to death . . . leave me alone—I want to die."

Andrew lowered his pistol and relaxed; the wounded soldier was no threat.

Somehow, some way . . . the wounded man must have read Andrew's body language and changed his mind.

The man raised up a little, and screamed, "Help me . . . please help me. I'm bleeding to death."

Approaching carefully, Andrew put his pistol into his waistband and offered the man a drink.

He appeared to be in his mid-twenties, thinner than average, with soiled yellow hair. He had a long beard that masked his true appearance. His threadbare Confederate uniform was filthy and torn in several places. He had no shoes. A soiled blanket roll was wrapped around his shoulder.

"Do you feel better now?" Andrew asked after the Reb had gulped down the remaining water from his canteen.

"How can I help you? Are you able to walk? Can you move at all?"

"No, I also sprained my ankle after taking a round in the arm, and I've lost too much blood . . . I'm too weak to move. Please, can you help me?"

Andrew thought, *Gramps told me this fighting would get worse. It has, but here I am in an unusual situation with a wounded, and probably dying, Rebel soldier, shot by a Yankee. What to do? I've got to do something.*

"Okay, listen up, here's what'll happen. Our brigade's medical facility is about 100 yards to the northeast. I've just been there with one of our wounded. Since you can't walk, I'll carry you, and our medics will do what they can to help. First, I need a little info. What's your name?"

He answered, "Joseph Reddick."

Ka-Boom!

"What?"

"Joseph Reddick . . . R-e-d-d-i-c-k, Reddick."

"Well, I'll be damned."

"What?"

"You'll never believe this. That's my Mom's and Gramp's last name, too. They both mentioned there were a lot of Reddicks in the South, only spelled with a double 'd' . . . I wonder if we're related somehow?"

Ka-Boom! More canister pellets rained down from the canopy above.

"Dang . . . let's get the heck out of here. Some of those rounds are landing too far beyond the line for comfort. I think your cannons are trying to reach over the lines to quartermaster and medical."

Without comment, Andrew picked Joe up, wrestled him over his shoulder, and struggled his way through the downed timber and rubble like a man afire. On the way, several rounds whistled overhead while he zig-zagged to the medical tent.

The medical officer at the brigade tent stopped Andrew. "Hold it right here! What's this? What have you got there, soldier? It looks like Johnny Reb to me . . . explain yourself!"

Andrew explained who he was, his unit, and the circumstances leading to the Rebel being brought to the Yankee medical unit.

"Well now, you've certainly performed way beyond the call of duty today. We'll take the Rebel and see what we can do for him. I suggest that you'd better get back to your unit—no telling whether our lines can hold. Lee has been throwing troops at us all day. They tell me we're holding. The slope up to the Union positions, called Cemetery Ridge, is littered with Rebel dead and dying. My advice to you is to—get! This is no place for a 14-year-old."

Andrew gave Joe one last look to say goodbye, but by then he had passed out either from pain or loss of blood. It was clear to Andrew that he had to get back to Company Headquarters—quickly. As he turned to leave, he stopped and yelled, "By the way, his name is Joe . . . Joe Reddick, that's with two 'd's'. He may even be a relative. My Gramp is a Redick, but with one d. Interesting, huh?"

The medical personnel listened passively to this seemingly unimportant connection . . . and repeated: "Get!" He then added that Frank was doing fine.

Just after clearing the medical area, Andrew found the path back to the 75th and ran full tilt.

Ka-Boom!

An aerial canister burst overhead and rained pellets down on Andrew.

A jagged pellet hit him on the side of his head. It threw him off his feet and slammed him onto the littered ground. His pistol went one way, his canteen another, and his hat a third. His ever-present bugle wrapped around his body and fell underneath him as he rolled over and crashed into a downed log.

He quickly felt his body parts for any broken or fractured bones. He found none, but did feel the blood running down his face from a tear in the skin above his left ear.

"Damn, that pellet tore a pretty big hole in my skin, and I think another pellet may have punctured my bugle. Thank you, old horn, you may have saved my life. I'm lucky the hit on the head didn't tear my ear off. The medical personnel were right, the Rebs are targeting support units *behind* the lines—or are just bad shots. That is awful, but as Wes said, 'war is hell' and just about *anything* goes."

He decided to cleanse the wound himself, wrap it to stop the bleeding, and move out of the area as quickly as possible. He could use the first aid kit at headquarters to do a better job later.

"Wait, where's my pistol, my hat? I'd better go back and get 'em. I've got to get out of this impact area, but I've also got to retrieve that gun.

He ran back, suddenly feeling a headache coming on from the wound, and searched for the big log that he had crashed into.

Ka-Boom!

Pellets riddled the area and splintered the overhead limbs.

Ka-Boom!

Just as he turned to leave, a canister burst at a lower level, throwing him to the ground. As he fell, he put his hands over his head . . . and got so low, he ate dirt in the process. It happened again. A pellet, ricocheting off a nearby rock, slammed into his right shoulder blade with a thud. It felt as though he had been hit with a ten-pound hammer. Painfully, he reached around slowly and found a blood-soaked pellet embedded in his back. His thick jacket had helped to lessen the impact on his flesh. He looked at it with contempt, but kept it as an example of a "lucky pellet," for if it had been a direct hit, versus a ricochet . . . he would have been killed.

He knew he had to move and leave the impact area. So, despite being in great pain, he rose slowly and continued his route to the 75th.

There was no running this time, nor zig-zagging to avoid in-coming rounds, no high stepping, leaning over freshly-downed trees; he carefully advanced using a slow, staggering off-balance crouch. One hand was on his wound above his ear, the bugle thrown over his back, and the pistol in his other hand. He felt pretty sure there would not be any more Rebels lost behind Yankee lines, but—one never knew in the chaos, the terror, the horror of war, what might pop-up unexpectedly.

At camp, he cleansed, disinfected, and dressed his head wound. He checked the horses on the picket line, looked to see if any rounds had hit the wagons—they had not—and thought of Frank. He thought, *Maybe I should have stopped in to see him when I dropped Joe off. Oh well, there had been too many incoming wounded to linger there, and the medical personnel said he was doing fine. That's okay by me.*

Andrew finally sat down to rest and noticed how banged up his bugle had gotten. The flared horn end was bent a full 45 degrees to the right and the mouthpiece 45 degrees in the other direction. It did not look very melodic. He chuckled at the twisted musical piece of brass . . . until he noticed a hole torn through the flared end. "Holy-cow! There's a large tear in the metal on one side of the flared end, and a big dent on the other side."

He put his finger through the hole, "Damn, I think my bugle may have saved my life . . . I'in indeed a lucky guy.

"Guess what? I'm not going to straighten it. It's earned its shape . . . through my travels and my falls. It has earned its battle scars. Then again, Wilson will probably make me straighten it, we'll see. I'll blow a few notes to see how she sounds."

Da-da . . . da-da-da . . . da-da-da-daaaaa.

*   *   *

As Andrew tested his bugle, several heads turned in the medical compound. "What's that?" a medical orderly said as the sound wafted through the air like a rhythmic tattoo.

A patient, Frank DeSellua, from the 75th, said, "That's our bugler; he's the boy who brought me in about an hour ago."

*   *   *

Back at the 75th, Andrew commented, "She sounds good. I may not straighten her until I'm told to—by Wilson. I'd better stay put awhile, it sounds like the offensive probe by the Rebs has failed. The excitement I hear in the ranks sure sounds like Yankee cheers—thank God—I think it may be over soon."

*   *   *

Wes looked at Wilson through the clearing smoke and exclaimed, "I think it's over . . . thank God. Longstreet's last advance has failed; the Rebels are retreating—at least for the day. Hurrah."

Wilson agreed. "'Tis true, Wes. Johnny Reb is in full retreat. The 75th has held. We stood alone with their final rush . . . and held our ground. We held for many reasons: sheer guts under fire; leadership by officers and NCO's, and an ample supply of fire power and ammo."

Wes looked at Wilson. "Speaking of ammo, I wonder how Frank is doing? Remember, Andrew made the ammo run after Frank was hurt. I'd better check on him. It looks like the fighting is over for the day.

"Speaking of Andrew, did you hear that?"

A distant bugle sang faintly . . . A familiar. sound, varying in strength, a rhythmic beating and rapping coming from the east. Someone was blowing a few notes as if to test a bugle. As quickly as it started, the sound abruptly stopped.

Wes commented, "It's gratifying to hear that sound. Wouldn't you agree that it sounds like Andrew? Like he's checking out his horn—testing it for some reason?"

"Wes, I think you're correct, Andrew's our boy . . . or more correctly, after today's trial under fire, he's the *man* from the 75th, who happens to blow the bugle, too."

MY HORSE, CHICO

An Essay

It all started in the 1940s, while going to the Allen Park theater every Saturday afternoon. As I recall, my brothers and I sat there four hours watching two main features (always the case at that time), coming attractions, several comical features (yep, The Road Runner), and, of course, WWII news from the front, and Edward R. Murrow reporting from London. I'm sure the latter was presented since television wasn't in most homes until the early 1950s. I'm not sure when the theaters stopped showing two features, maybe the 1960s.

Check this out: With two features, many patrons only stayed

for one, or, in our case, Mom said we had to leave when one of the films of questionable character was shown. That was hard to do. You know, we'd ask, "Wonder what neat stuff we're missing. Sex? Violence?" In late afternoon, we'd leave the theater with dilated eyes so big we couldn't see for several minutes. Each of us had a quarter, 14 cents for a ticket, the rest spent on candy, like, Dots, NECCO Wafers, and Black Crows.

You may ask: "What's all this leading to? Isn't this about a horse called Chico?"

Okay. Over the years, there were various genera shown: horror, mystery, romance, and, my favorite, westerns. In fact, fifty percent of the features were westerns. I had my heroes who rode beautiful horses chasing the bad men of the west. Roy Rogers rode a palomino named Trigger; The Lone Ranger sat astride a white horse called Silver, yelling, "Hi ho, Silver, away!" Tonto, the Ranger's Indian side kick, rode a pinto named Scout. His favorite saying was, "Get 'em up, Scout!" All good cowboys, like Tom Mix, Lash LaRue, and Hopalong Cassidy, rode beautiful horses. I can guarantee you the bad guys rode haggard-looking mustangs—by plan. Matter of fact, the dress of the bad guys was haggard, too.

On another level, of course, were the classic films like National Velvet, with Mickey Rooney, Liz Taylor playing Velvet Brown, riding her horse, called The Pie, in steeplechase event. Then there was Black Beauty, another film that showcased beautiful horses. As such, I became a horse guy—fell in love with that four-legged beauty. Don't get me wrong, I still built model airplanes, played ball, and biked every road in Allen Park, but the animal I loved most, I could not have. We lived in town, so I was satisfied with a beautiful German Shorthaired Pointer we called Fritz. I loved that dog. But I loved horses, too.

When we were visiting farms, I'd watch them for hours, and whenever possible, feed and curry them. In the 1950s, every other farm still had a team, some working, others kept for sentimental value. Dad, at some expense, took all three of us boys horseback riding once a year. I remember those times at a ranch in Taylor, north of Allen Park, and another near Bay Crest—by Grandma Broome's cottage. Dad always said if I saved my money and learned how to take care of horses, I could get one when we moved to a farm. The future looked good. Right?

Wrong.

Since 1948, we'd been scouring the lower half of Michigan for a farm we could afford. It was 1950 and we still could not find the right one, at the right price, in the right place. Geez, I was getting older—I'd turn 13 that coming April. Darn!

Then it happened.

We Bought a farm south of Ypsilanti that winter and would be moving in the spring.

I was on cloud nine for months. Dad raised me higher in the clouds by quietly buying a used saddle, surprising me with it on my birthday. Yep, I bought saddle soap, and cleaned up that beautiful piece of formed leather. I also rolled a blanket in a rain slicker, tied it on the rear of the saddle, and made a storage rack for it. That way, I could keep it in the bedroom I shared with my brothers, Dave and Milt. That ended quickly as the room started smelling like a tack room. Darn brothers. "Breathe through your mouths," I told them. For my aggressiveness, they hid my saddle for a day. Later Mom interceded on my behalf and pinned their ears back.

After a year on the farm, working long hours to get crops planted as soon as possible, I still did not have my horse. So I talked to Dad and Mom. It was a good talk. I learned sweat equity on my part, meaning I needed to work a little longer and harder on the start-up operation with our new farm. Plus, I learned another term, called cash flow. They were honest enough to say there was at least a year's delay on receipts/profits from the first year's grain and hay sales. As a luxury item, the horse would have to wait. I guess being 14 meant I was old enough to understand. They were right. I worked hard, and silently waited for the right time. I knew it would come.

It happened again.

At dinner one evening, Dad made a subtle comment on getting a good night's sleep since we were going to an Ann Arbor pasture to help our cattle buyer, Honey Konchel, round up some cattle. Honey was a classic 20th century wrangler. He chewed tobacco, wore cowboy boots, denim, a beat-up John Wayne-type hat, and carried a big trucker's wallet—like a biker—in his rear pocket. Some claimed that wallet was his office. We liked the guy for several reasons: he bought cattle for Dad at a good price, he let us borrow some of his farm equipment, and he let us help him round up cattle several times a year. What's so neat about that? After round-up, he'd give us twenty dollars and say, "Go to the store and buy lunch for us—and get yourselves something special, too. Like on a holiday, we bought the best lunch meat, cheese, rolls, bread, pies, and jars of jam and peanut butter. We topped it all with a couple six-packs of root beer and milk. It was always a grand time running, dodging, and out-smarting cattle reluctant to be corralled.

The four of us rode in Honey's stock truck to the pasture, and we helped him back up to the loading chute. Then we took off to find the herd on the 160 acres. It didn't take long. We saw them lying down in a shaded area near a creek. Puzzled as we looked out over the area, it appeared as though a horse, a beautiful pinto, was standing nearby. He probably had wandered into Honey's area recently. Oh well, I thought. We can cut him from the herd. Suddenly, Honey and Dad said to hold back a little and walk with them.

I said to Dave, "How boring. We'd rather run, right?"

Rather than agree with me, Dave gave a passive facial response.

Then it happened again.

Honey said, "Look out there, son, by the herd. You see that pinto?"

I told him I saw it.

"I would like you to be the owner."

Shocked, I hollered, "What? You mean it's ours?"

"No, Son, it's yours."

You can imagine how I felt about Dad, Honey, and even Dave, who, by the look on his face knew about the horse.

As you might have guessed, our next job was to separate the horse from the herd and get him into the corral and on the stock truck.

There he was, close up and personal, as we drove him along the fence line to the corral. His markings were a mixture of black and brown on white, with a solid white tail and stockings. He looked beautiful and courageous as he slipped right by us near the corral.

Out we went again, to get him up to the corral from another direction, only to have him leap by us with a vengeance of a warrior in battle. I wondered, is this the tame horse Honey talked of, the horse I'd have no trouble riding?

I'll make a long story short by saying, we had that horse close to the corral gate two more times and he ran right through us. He knew very well what was going to happen. He was going to lose his freedom of the range, his freedom from man. Not that man was bad, but he'd be under saddle and wearing a bit when he'd rather be left alone. But we all do things at time we'd rather not. I vowed to make his life enjoyable.

Tired, Honey said, "If we don't get him in the corral this (third) time, we'll come back another day." Thus bringing the three-hour ordeal to an end.

I whispered to Dave, "We've got to do it. Dad won't stay much longer."

We got him on that last try. Maybe he was tired. We actually sacrificed our bodies at the corral's gate by holding hands as if we were a chain link fence. Honey let me know that I owed him a six pack for the day playing cowboy. I did more than that. Dad bought him a case.

Back at the farm, I rode that pinto daily, curried him after each ride, and gave him a giant's portion of molasses and oats. Chico seemed to be a good name, meaning kid or boy in Spanish. In any case, I liked it for my pinto.

One day, I was holding his head up with the halter rope, and sure enough, he surprised me by performing the stretch position. In doing so, he put both forelegs forward and rear legs back. It was stunning to see him hold that position until I released him.

"Dang," I mumbled. "He knows tricks, too."

Yeah, he threw me once. Well, not quite; we were galloping across a field and all of a sudden he stopped. I flew over his head and crashed in front of him. Unhurt, I looked around for a reason for his abrupt halt. I found no reason at all. Oh, well. If that's the worse toss over the years, I guess I was pretty lucky—or he was just a well-mannered horse. I tend to believe the latter.

He performed as a true friend for years until I had to go away to school. We sold him to another young man to care for and love. Thankfully, I had my day in the sun. Every night, before turning in, I'd go to the stall or barnyard, wherever he was, and I'd say good night while he chewed on the apple I'd brought for him.

SAILING TO NASSAU

An Essay

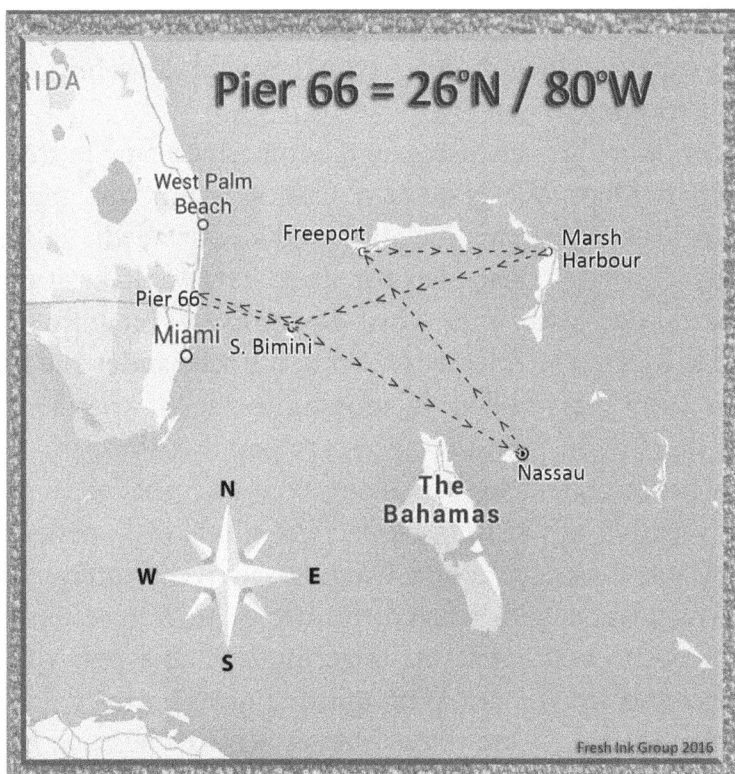

Pier 66 = 26°N / 80°W

In the late 1950s, brother Dave and a few Betas from the University of Michigan got together with me and my roommate Frank at Eastern Michigan University, with an exciting idea to really do something special on spring break. Their idea was to sail to Nassau in the Bahamas and explore the archipelago's various inhabited and uninhabited islands. They would lease a sail boat with a small motor. Their thinking was: with adequate accommodations aboard for a crew of six, there would be no need for the expense of motel and restaurant fees in the islands. Many thought the plan was far-fetched and risky. In fact, several who were interested at first dropped out, but were quickly replaced by a more adventuresome lot. Preliminary estimates indicated each of the six crew members' cost would be five-hundred dollars. After several weeks, six prevailed, the crew was assembled and began work to obtain a captain, since no boat owner would lease his craft to a bunch of rookies.

Sure enough, he was discovered, after advertising in the Naval Engineering Dept. We got lucky, Chuck Smith was anxious to join us. A licensed captain, he answered all our needs, and he immediately drafted a float plan for us to review. It basically presented a ten-day lease, with a two-day cruise to New Providence Island. He located an adequate boat in a Fort Lauderdale marina. It was a 1950 glass-hulled 46-foot motor sailor with ketch rig. Moving quickly, he sent the necessary paperwork to the broker, signed a contract, and we had a bare boat in April for 10 days.

Our meeting at the Beta House was a real eye-opener for all of us—in more ways than one. Chuck took over from my brother Dave, who originally organized the trip. Chuck gave us reading assignments on boating terms covering several aspect of sailing both large and small craft. With a little humor in his voice and a wry smile, he said, "One thing I never want to hear on board is the word *rope*, like 'Toss me the *rope*.'" On board, a rope is a *line*, the rope to raise the sail is a *halyard*, and the rope to trim the sail is the *sheet*. Got it?

He went on to discuss other nautical terms such as: beam, forestay, shrouds, jib, and battens. There were also directions on the boat: port, starboard, fore, and aft. He mentioned that the ketch rig was indeed unique with two masts, a mainsail at midships, and a mizzen behind the helm.

He had arranged for the broker to move the boat—which we agreed to name *Windward*—by motor to Pier 66 south of Fort

Lauderdale; it's a less congested port and a straight easterly shot to New Providence Island.

On the way back to the dorm, Frank admitted that he had a few questions but was embarrassed to ask. Not to worry, I told him. I'd guess many of us had questions of our own. I think Chuck's assertive, demanding persona in speaking mechanically, without intonation, was in part to project to us the seriousness of our plan, and that sailing the Atlantic in April is not for the weak hearted. Yes, he said there were sharks galore on the Bahaman banks, but reminded us that the Portuguese Man-O-War is more dangerous to a swimmer. He also mentioned the barbed toxic tail on the Manta Ray is lethal.

Upon arriving at Pier 66, on Monday, Chuck gave us a tour of the boat. He repeated terms (smiled at the rope reference) and reviewed operations. We did a shakedown cruise due east in the Atlantic at dusk, and after returning to port, Chuck announced that we's be leaving 1900 hours, so get all our stuff aboard.

"What?" Frank exclaimed. "Tonight?"

I said, "It appears the plan works out this way."

Chuck reviewed the first portion of the float plan of two days to New Providence, and noted our first sail would be to the Bi-mini Islands, at about 52 miles due east at 92 degrees, where we'd drop anchor for an overnighter. It is too dangerous to pass through at night, with our draft at five feet due to our fixed keel. At 52 miles and a hull speed of 9 knots, we'd be there in six hours, arriving 0100 hours Tuesday.

Chuck had us all check to make sure our sleeping bags were on *Windward*, that we had sunglasses, billed caps, Coppertone sun tanning lotion, and cars locked.

At 1900 hours, after motoring to clear the break wall, we raised sails, and set a course 92 degrees east. Trimming the jib, mainsail, and mizzen, we all hugged the rail as we sliced through the water.

I looked back at the lights of Miami and Fort Lauderdale framing the setting sun over the good old U.S.A. Soon we'd be in the commonwealth of Great Britain, under rules and regulations of the Crown.

"Dang," I said, "I hope the boys behave and know the different rules and regulations outside the States. I'd hate to have an international incident."

Frank broke my thoughts, saying, "This is better than I could have ever imagined."

He edged over to Chuck and asked how he knew we'd arrive at the Bimini Straits with our azimuth at 92 degrees east, when we're sailing across the strong Gulf Stream pushing northward at a good clip.

Chuck explained we had a knot indicator and charts, plus a radio beacon on Bimini that we'd be able to zero in on, and when close, we'd spot the light code on the buoy near the straits.

"Code light?" Frank asked.

All navigation aids have a Morse Code signal of blinking lights and sound indicating which buoy is where. The Bimini buoy is letter B (__ . . ./DAH-DIT-DIT-DIT) 24/7.

Half way to Bimini, Chuck called for the first watch. Dave took the helm. After a quick briefing, Chuck went below for some shut-eye. The only cues he gave Dave was on trimming the sails if the wind changed direction.

As the crew enjoyed the first night on the Atlantic, Dave noted that he really enjoyed manning the helm. He mentioned later that the feeling at the helm was a mixture of complete control, like a CFO, like a father or lover, knowing that many factors are under his direct control—a feeling of strength.

Being his brother, I was pleased that he found solace at the helm.

Looking up at the billowing sails racing through the starlit sky, we all felt a little more nautical after Chuck explained how *Windward's* sails propelled us through the luminescent sea. He'd said, "The sail is like a vertical airplane wing." Using his hands as a teaching aide, he continued, "The convex surface of the sail is like the upper curved portion of a wing. This is the area where the air moves slower than the bottom, creating *lift*—in our case, *thrust*. Gentlemen, you've just learned one of our basic physical laws used often in travel: *The Bernoulli Effect*."

At 2000 hours, the end of Dave's watch, Chuck took the helm as we approached Bimini and the buoy marking entry into the strait. He asked the crew to take notice as he came about to a luff, putting *Windward* dead in the water. We dropped anchor, turned on the mast light (indicating boat at anchor) and had a quick crew meeting where he showed us the next course to Nassau. This leg will be about 120 nautical miles, or about 13 hours, depending on wind direction and velocity. Everyone had a snack and sang some nautical songs with John on guitar. At 2400 hours, Frank took the midnight watch as others crashed in the bags while listening to the melodic lapping of waves against the hull. It was music to our ears when the slapping of the halyards to their mast joined in with the groans of the anchor line as it fought its cleat on the bow. In the most liberal description: a symphony of sounds over the sea.

Day two (Tuesday) found us underway at 0600 hours as we slipped through the narrow passage of the Bimini atoll, heading southeast on our long leg to Nassau.

After the sails were set and trimmed, Chuck determined the winds were too moderate for maximum hull speed. He started the little motor to give us 9 knots.

Everyone was perched on the rail as we sailed on a beam reach. Taking a double watch, Chuck explained a little about New Providence, the Pilot House where we'd arranged docking, and the sights to see while there—though only for a day. He explained we'd be island hopping during the week, returning to Nassau prior to departure.

Those on deck were either fishing or waving at the gals on passing yachts. Others were taking pictures of the dolphins playing tag in our wake.

They talked about going to the Fish Market, government buildings, and the infamous British Colonial Hotel, the very place the queen and her family stay. John asked if they anticipated any problems from customs. No one seemed to have contraband—except for Ron's thirty-thirty Winchester Carbine. That would certainly be declared and locked up until we moved out.

"Anybody have hard drugs in their possession?" Frank asked.

Silence.

"I guess that means none."

We docked at the Pilot House, cleared customs (they took Ron's gun) and were check superficially for alcohol and drugs, before gaining permission to explore their islands.

That night we celebrated with a native drink containing rum, Coke, pineapple, and limes, in what is called a Tribute to Nassau. After a few of these iced bullets, we all turned in.

Day three (Wednesday) found everyone busy cleaning the deck with fresh water (salt water becomes sticky), topping off the water and fuel tanks, cleaning and getting ready to sail. Chuck insisted on this procedure, even though we were going to tour Nassau that day. He always wanted the boat ready to sail at a moment's notice—in case of emergency.

We all went ashore—except the man on watch—and sure enough, after checking out the political buildings, The British Colonial, and the Fish Market, a few returned with girls in tow to see the boat. Kind of crowded below, the gals kicked the guys out and fixed a meal for all ten. After singing local songs from their school, it was determined Michigan's fight song, "Hail to the Victors," was the best of the lot, by vote of 7 to 3. After telling stories (some true) into the night, at midnight, wearing less clothing than when boarding, the gals left carrying some of the wet clothes and heels. A good time was had by all. Dave commented as they left the boat, "So that's what a thong bathing suit looks like."

Day four (Thursday) found the crew heading out to explore Grand Bahama Island to the northwest. After docking and touring the local fish markets and notable historic buildings (Columbus docked here in the 1500s), we visited Freeport on the north coastline, one of the largest towns in the islands. Nightlife was so unique at a little club in the center of the island—a native club, meaning native music—they stayed over and crashed on the boat in Freeport.

Day five (Friday) Chuck found the dockage and the fellow yachtsman so accommodating at Freeport, he arranged for the entire crew to go fishing in the morning with a few of the fishing charters, in trade for a sail on the *Windward* that evening. As such, it was an exciting day for all seven of the crew, some of which were going through alcohol withdrawal. They fished for grouper, shark (yes, they're eaten), and striped bass. With four on one boat and three on the other, there was a contest as to who caught the most poundage. *Big Boy* charter won with an easy pick since it had caught a six-foot hammerhead shark.

That's another story.

While trying to land the bugger, a fisherman fell in and, for a second, was thrashing around with hammerhead, until he cleared the boat. Believe me, he could have walked on water at that time. If there's one shark, you just know he has buddies lurking nearby. He got back in the boat in seconds, not minutes.

Day six (Saturday) we headed due east to Grand Abaco and its town, Marsh Harbor. An industrialized town, it also had many yacht harbors since it was the starting point for sailing or motoring across the Atlantic to Bermuda or Europe. The locals say the difference between Grand Bahama and Grand Abaco is 100 feet longer and one million times more expensive. Yep, we're talking yachts so big they have a permanent crew of 4 to 6 for year-round motoring or sailing to Europe, South America, or North America. Some just follow the weather and you might find one on Lake Michigan in July and the Bahamas in December. We had a good time hob-knobbing among the rich, and took off that night for Nassau.

Day Seven and eight (Sunday and Monday). Land lubbers for the next two days, we explored the island with little more interest in the local culture and found one of the exclusive native clubs called *The Cat and the Fiddle.* The local music was stunning, the dances out of this world, and the dancers world-class. We saw limbo dancers lower their bodies to less than a foot off the ground. Our best was two feet. It made me wonder if these dancers really had any bones.

Check this out. On our last night, we rented a Singer auto to go inland. This little two-seater (British car), like a MG TD-3, is like a toy. So, here we are, seven of us on the seats, fenders, running boards and whatever, and as we head out of town, we run into one of the local constables. Six foot six, black as coal, and dressed to the nines. He's standing in the middle of the road with his white feathered pith helmet, white tunic, black pants, and red sash, with his hand out, indicating that we should STOP!

We thought we had it. Bloody well, in the lock-up on our last night. As we started to off-load the little car, he said, "No problem, man. Enjoy yourselves. I stopped you because you forgot to turn on your lights." He motioned for us to pass and we, for some reason, saluted him as we drove by.

Another fine day found us crashing on *Windward* with Chuck going over the float plan for our return to civilization. We'd soon return to real life in the good old U.S.A.

Day nine and ten (Tuesday and Wednesday). Now that we considered ourselves seasoned sailors, the trip home was uneventful as we sailed through Bimini Straits and back to Pier 66.

The layered experiences made an indelible mark on our lives. To the Spirit of the sea, we thank you for safe passage.

Besides Dave inviting me on this sailing adventure, he also flew me to California in the later '50s. We toured the state's attractions and visited Mexico, too. The local culture of Tijuana and the bullfights made a lasting impression in my life.

Thanks, Dave.

AWAY ALL BOATS

An Essay

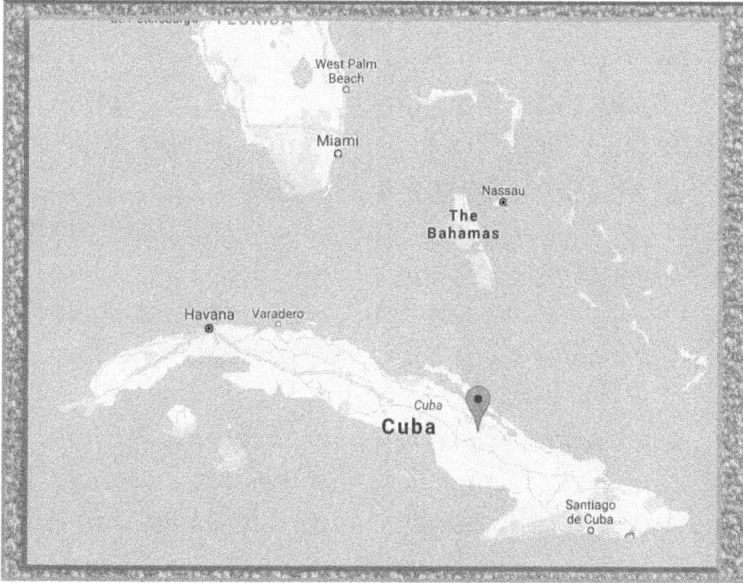

The Cuban Missile Crisis thrust two of the most powerful nations in the world on the brink of WWIII. For younger readers, in the early 1960s the Soviet Union came to the aid of the failing dictatorship of Fidel Castro, Cuba's revolutionary leader. They provided various trade items like petroleum, food stuffs, and financial aid in exchange for sugar. Providing military support received little notice until they started delivering short and long range missiles. The construction of the sites was noticed by random fly-overs and tourist accounts. The activity was clearly a violation of SALT II (Strategic Arms Limitations Treaty) by the Soviets. Also, the U.S. was not going to allow the Soviets to establish a foothold in the Western Hemisphere with missiles.

President Kennedy immediately drew the line on this activity and started diplomatic discussion with Soviet Premier Khrushchev. To demonstrate to the Soviets how serious their move, Kennedy directed the Joint Chiefs of Staff to develop a contingency plan for the invasion of Cuba if diplomacy failed. The U.S. was not going to allow Soviet missiles 80 miles to the south of Florida.

The results were immediate. A Joint Task Force (JTF) was formed of Army, Navy, Air Force, and Marines, with a mission to invade, occupy, and dismantle any missiles on the island. The effort would be called Operation Sea Wall.

Okay so far, but what's the point here? All this is history, you may be thinking. Allow me to explain.

Being a young Lieutenant in the Army Security Agency, Communications Intelliegence (gathering) Battalion, assigned to the 82nd Airborne Division, I was directed to report with four Voice Intercept and Jamming (VIJ) teams, which included four enlisted and one sergeant per team, to the 4th Division, Ft. Lewis, Tacoma, Washington. As part of the JTF, our unit would start training at Ft. Lewis and support the Brigade Commander of the 4th with our intelligence capabilities (both voice and code comm). There, I learned, Operation Sea Wall would be an amphibious assault with naval ships including the infamous aging 30-foot LCVP (Landing Craft Vehicle Personnel) carried to the launch site by several 300-foot APA (All Purpose Assault) ships. It sounded much like the Allied landings in France (D-Day) in 1945, and the landings at Inchon, Korea, by MacArthur in 1951. It looked like we were going to be part of history in the making. In fact, rumor had it that this would be the last time this type of assault would be used. Why? The LCVP, as well as the PT Boat (Patrol Torpedo) manufactured by J.C. Higgins, had been fabricated in the 1940s by the only material available at the time: marine plywood. Yes, plywood. (Aluminum was used for aircraft during the war.) Plywood had a life span of 25 years, which seemed adequate, and construction was outstanding. But, if you do the math, that was 20 years earlier. I'd heard many of the seams and joints had been fiberglassed recently, and many of the old reliable Gray Marine flat-head six engines were on their last legs—on their last cycle! Thankfully, the front ramp for loading and unloading personnel and equipment was metal.

Can you imagine how a soldier during the D-Day landing must have felt as he was about to unload onto the beach? All he hears prior to that time is the sound of gun fire and the *ping* of those rounds bouncing off the metal ramp.

We trained on land, learning the proper way to go over the side via cargo nets, hanging 30 feet down the side of the ship. Then we'd step into little boats. I can tell you from personal experience that it is nothing like going over into the boat in rough seas. Everyone has something to carry. It might be a weapon or a radio or a sea bag slung over his shoulder. And there are others on either side, below, and coming down on you if you hesitate. Your next encounter is the upward and downward movement of the boat in typical sea swells—sometimes up to four feet, which isn't fun. However, per training, no one was to help him. Why? You had to clear the net since more are following. An individual just could not hold up the boat from its planned dwell time. The only thing you could do is struggle around him, and in time he'll climb down when he sees it is better getting into the boat rather than getting into the Pacific, since he certainly couldn't remain in the net. It is always best to discover these problems in training.

Much to my surprise, the maneuver site was San Juan Island, a U.S. National Park, about the size of Cuba, in the San de Fuca Straits, an inlet from the Pacific just off Vancouver, B.C. There were a few sheep herders and scenic attractions, but otherwise sparsely populated. With the intense training complete, troops and equipment loaded, we weighed anchor and headed out of the straits into the Pacific to rendezvous with other elements of the assault force.

During planning at sea with the Brigade Commander, I had a chance to communicate with my men who had loaded our ¾ ton vehicles and equipment on a LCD (Landing Craft Dock) whose clamshell-like bow opened up on shore to discharge its cargo. They reported everything was secure and coordination with the assault troops complete. They then teased me that they would ride off onto shore in the vehicles versus going over the side on the cargo net. "Not funny," I replied.

I made a few errors aboard ship. Not being familiar with some shipboard customs, I berthed in the wrong staterooms, staying in the one reserved for Captains, not Lieutenants; and when I asked why the evening film was not being shown as we were all sitting there, quietly I was told by the EXO, "We do not start until the Captain of the ship is seated." Likewise, I was told not to clear my own dishes while in *officer country*. That's a job for which they hire others. So I went outside to the rail and witnessed a beautiful sunset on the Pacific, unobstructed by man. Of all the activities aboard this huge ship, this moment, which I'd have liked to share with my wife, made the most lasting impression of the short hours sailing with the Navy.

The operation started at 0600 hours the next morning with all hands on deck.

After the Air Force simulated neutralizing the island defenses, and the Marines secured the beachhead, the Navy deck hands started lowering the LCVPs over the side. Their movements were like a well-planned dance as the boats circled on either side of the ship until all were launched. Then a speaker barked, "All over the side." Troops went down the cargo nets on both sides of the ship. After taking on 20 to 25 men, the LCVP motored back to the circle and another moved in quickly to be loaded. Upon completion, the 10 boats on either side lined up in a row of skirmishers with alternating separation and headed for the beach when the officer on deck barked, "Away all boats."

No one spoke until the host operator said, "Better keep your head down, Lieutenant. We're about to take on some water."

I answered, "Will do." No sooner had the words left my mouth we grounded out on the beach. The front ramp crashed into the surf and the operator yelled for us to get out on the double. Wet to the knees, my next job was to find our ASA unit unloading from the LSD down the beach. Our instructions were clear: don't linger. There were many other units coming ashore.

Lucky for me, I found all our units, they were assigned to the appropriate infantry headquarters and the operation was underway.

All the units moved about the island and intercepted (canned) enemy traffic—both voice and code. We were successful in supporting the infantry units.

Discipline was good, equipment worked well, and our mission was accomplished. We did have a little problem with the troops being hungry on the third day. Carrying only three days rations on their backs, some ate too much the first day and a rumor got to me later that a few of my own men were planning on butchering a sheep for dinner the third day. As a maneuver, it served our needs to get the kinks out of any operational plans prior to invading Cuba. Being an intelligence-gathering unit, we took no part in capturing the planted blue troops simulating Soviet technicians manning the missiles or deactivating the missile sites. We departed the island in a more traditional manner and boarded ship likewise. The only casualties on the island were four collapsed bridges, one burned oat field, and three dead sheep. No, my guys didn't do it; they were run over by fast moving vehicles at night.

Sea Wall was a success, but did it meet its second goal: a deterrent? I'm not sure anybody knows. We do know that the KGB followed our plans. The NSA (National Security Agency) saw them, and we heard them in the Vancouver area. They must have known Kennedy was serious. Why? Although cost is never a factor in a military operation, Gen. M. Taylor, who directed the operation, undauntedly reported later that it cost several million dollars, and the entire JTF was now headed to Homestead A.F.B. in Florida to regroup. While there, attorneys were issuing last will and testaments (SOP for combat), and quartermaster was issuing live ammunition. All leaves were cancelled and a DEFCON-One was called. He was serious. The JTF was now located 100 miles from Cuba, with C-119s (flying boxcars) aircraft awaiting airborne troops on the flight line.

Was the operation a deterrent? You answer the question. I say, "Yes." The show of force worked. The Soviets removed the missiles. WWIII was avoided.

The press credited the tough stance of Kennedy diplomacy for the Soviet *blink*. However, only the KGB and those who monitored Operation Sea Wall will ever know the full story.

Thankful that cooler heads prevailed, all units returned to their home base and remained in DEFCON-One. I was proud of my men and the men of the JTF for this experience. The impact was certainly in being on the team, but the one aspect that still lingers is knowing that our unit was the last to use the LCVP in an amphibious landing. I'm proud to have been in the last unit to hear the deck officer say, "Away All Boats."

A SHARED GARDEN

An Essay

Strolling to my garden plot one morning, I gazed eastward where the faint flush of dawn seeped crimson along the way. Adding to dawn's spectacle, a northerly breeze was blowing over the freshly filled earth making the air smell warm and mild. A dog barked upwind as if to welcome dawn, too. In addition to the dog's proclamation, while stealing through the dew-laden grass, I could also hear the low staccato beat of a "Jumping Johnny" John Deere tractor laboring downwind. It was truly a glorious morn.

Another slight sound caught my ear. Glancing to the west, I noticed a killdeer, a bird with a beautiful brown cape of feathers,

majors on a snow white breast, plus scattered black minors. She
was fluttering on her breast as with a broken wing. It was her well-
known built-in defense to draw adversaries away from her nesting
place. Her cry clearly said, "Chase me . . . catch me . . . I'm hurt .
. . follow me." I stood still to honor her efforts and shared a stare.
In time, thinking I had fallen for her ruse, she stood, regained her
proud comportment, her assertive motherly posture, and nerv-
ously flicked her tail feathers.

We talked. I welcomed her to my garden and also had a little
chat with her family . . . alone, and in the reflective mood telling
them I missed them and was sorry they were not there to share
the glorious morn. Then I recalled a similar morn, years ago, a
song to my first love . . . it was from the Song of Solomon:

> "Rise up, my love, my fair one, and come away. For lo, the
> winter is past, the rain is over and gone; the flowers appear
> on the earth; the time of the singing of birds is come . . . "

I hoped my words would soothe, pacify, calm . . . and convince her that I would not harm her or her nest wherever it was
located. After a short stalemate, she seemed to acknowledge that
I was not a threat, then continued her search for insects among
the freshly tilled breast of Mother Earth.

At my garden now, I discovered for the first time her primitive
nest and four beautiful beige eggs, speckled with various-sized
brown and black spots . . . the exact color of the soil at that location. Frankly, without her faux display of injury I may not have
seen the earthen nest for days. Luckily the eggs lay between the
cukes and garlic, safe, for now . . . and later, too, as future vines
would make for a cozy abode.

Mother approached me again, but before starting her broken
wing routine I assured her that I would work around her sacred
birthing spot. We talked again until it appeared she was convinced

that I meant no harm ... was it my body language? ... it certainly wasn't my English. Then again, it could have been the inflection of my words. Who knows? She seemed to understand my promise, my caring words, but she remained cautious and sat on the edge of the garden with her body language of a "doubting Thomas." Like any concerned Mother, she slanted, rotated, and leaned her head, looking to ensure that I had kept my word as we continued to chat.

With both of us settled now, suddenly her mate arrived with a burst of noisy fluttering bluster. He was naturally unsure of her predicament. A strong-willed peeping by her followed until finally relaxed. He settled down in short order and sat next to her in a loving, cooing fashion as I continued to till my plot ... now under the gaze of four eyes. While on my knees, just a few feet apart, it was as if we were a family, a trio, anticipating the big hatch. Yet, I knew I must move on so Mom could sit on her progeny and share the warmth of her breast.

While I finished my tasks, we talked a little more and, as if they understood, I announced that I was leaving and they both stood up and bobbed in place. I arose, and while turning to leave, Mom quickly scrambled to her nest and tucked her future chicks under her warm downy breast. As expected, in Nature's plan, the brown cape feathers concealed her presence very well. One final look gave me the pride of being a small part of an extended family ... at least for a few weeks.

As I stole away, shadows raced across the garden. The sun rose above the horizon, bathing the three of us in its wonder, Mom now content, Dad searching for insects for both. Leaving the area triggered a rustling in the trees as a flock of sparrows sailed to the grassy apron around my garden. Tranquility returned to the scene as I looked to Father Sun and thanked Him for the warmth He gave me and the winged creatures that shared our world ...

I am blessed.

WATER JOURNEY
Children's Fiction

The journey of a young Indian boy to visit a likable girl began many years ago. Several tribes of Indians lived on the shores of a series of large lakes. The tribal leaders provided a cheerful place for children to live and learn the ways of Earth Mother and Father Sky.

*   *   *

They called the boy Wind Spirit, sometimes shortened to

Windy. He was learning many tribal tasks. A young brave needed to learn how to survive in the wilderness. His father, Golden Bear, taught him the ways of the forest and the habits of the four-legged animals. Windy learned how to make hooks and spears to catch the finned, and weapons to capture the hooved and winged. All these skills would be important in his search for self-discovery—his Quest—while on an adventurous journey.

*   *   *

Just as important was the work performed by his mother, White Dove. She was in charge of the camp's daily activities. Wind Spirit was shown how the women prepared food, and how they selected healing plants from the forest and swamps. He learned to treat animal skins with tanning solutions that changed them to beautiful leather and pelts. He was shown how women of the tribe sewed many types of leather together to make shoes, pants, and decorative shields. White Dove also showed him how she weaved yarn into clothing on a loom.

She showed him how to make soap, which was highly valued. Very few knew how to make it from animal fat and fire ash. Being part plant and part animal, it seemed as if it were almost alive. While his mother washed clothes for the family, Wind Spirit often bathed nearby. Sometimes he talked to his soap as if a friend.

*   *   *

One day, Wind Spirit sat alone on the river bank, washing up after cleaning a deer hide. He daydreamed of the charming Indian girl, Raven Maiden, who lived downriver. He had met her on a trip to her village earlier in the year. Wind Spirit wanted to be with her again, but he was too young to leave camp alone. Still thinking of her, he washed the tanning liquids off his body. Suddenly he felt a rush of wind from the river, followed by a bright light.

*   *   *

Holding his hand up to his eyes to shield the glare, Wind Spirit saw what looked like a "spirit being" hovering over the water. It raised its hands and spoke: "I have heard your wish. You are a good young man, so I will answer your request. There is a way to let Raven Maiden know your feelings for her. I will tell her that you will visit her soon with a gift of soap. The gift will be special, since the soap was made by your own hands. It is indeed a personal present. What happens next will be up to her. Go in peace, my son."

"But. . . Ah. . . How. . . ?" Wind Spirit mumbled.

The spirit form vanished as quickly as it appeared.

*　　*　　*

Not expecting an answer, Windy stood in silence, in wonder of The Spirit's visit. He thought, *Mom and Dad told me that The Great Spirit visits His people in times of need. I guess I'm a very lucky boy.* He picked up the soap and described to it what had happened. Windy put the large, pearl-gray bar of soap in his pack. He gathered up his tanning tools and hide. He looked down the river one more time, and ran back to camp.

*　　*　　*

Wind Spirit told his mother everything that happened.

Based on her wisdom of many moons, White Dove told him, "The Great Spirit acts in mysterious ways. The spirit may have big plans for you. Remember, the soap is indeed a living part of Earth. By taking the soap to the girl, The Spirit may be providing you with some problem-solving experiences. It may be a test of your ability to survive hardships."

"But Mom, I have no way to travel down the river."

"True, my son, but with the skills you have learned from your dad, I'm sure you will find a way."

He thought about it and remembered his father showing him

how to make a raft. "Yes! I'll make a very good raft!"

Very quickly, Wind Spirit built a raft of logs, and tied the soap on it. He asked his Mother, "Isn't it risky to float down the river? There are many dangers along the way."

"True, my son, but do not worry. Although you are very young, you should go. The Great Spirit will find a way to be at your side and help you. Sometimes He appears to us as a raven."

*   *   *

Wind Spirit drifted along the banks of the river. He floated past large rocks, beautiful pines, and pleasing sandy shores. As he paddled with a single oar, he kept checking the ties holding the soap.

Little by little, the current slowed, then almost stopped. He drifted into a beautiful, smooth pool. He came to a complete stop at the far end where a dam crossed the river. Windy caught his breath and thanked the Great Spirit for a safe journey. He rested, but not for long. A series of small waves led to very fast rockin'-and-rollin' waves. He rubbed the water from his eyes and looked around. He was being held captive by the current on the dam of a beaver pond. Worse yet, two playful young beaver kits were headed his way.

*   *   *

Treating Wind Spirit's raft as if a toy, the kits pushed him back and forth. They separated more and more to see how far they could push the raft between them. Losing interest in the game, the beaver kits started rocking the raft.

"Yikes!" Wind Spirit yelled, "I hope they're not going to tip me over!" Luckily, Mother Beaver called for the kits to leave the raft alone. Seeing the bar of soap, she asked if she could use it for her daily wash.

He answered, "Of course."

Mother Beaver washed her clothes, and returned the soap with a big "Thank you."

Wind Spirit made his way slowly to the edge of the dam. Giggling, the kits suddenly pushed the raft over. He coasted safely into the current below. "Hooray!" he shouted.

He got the break he needed to escape the playful young beaver kits.

*   *   *

Wind Spirit noticed that the soap was rounder and smaller now. Still, he smiled after the tiring time in the pond. The downriver current effortlessly weaved him between large boulders. Many of them displayed Native Indian drawings of deer, bear, the sun, and other symbols. He enjoyed the warmth of the sunshine, and took pleasure in his time alone as he traveled Earth Mother's waters. Soon he floated under low-hanging branches covering the river. The sun was partially blocked as he entered the arch-shaped overhanging trees. In the dark shadows, he found himself in a swampy section of the river. Some of the branches were so low the leaves rubbed against his body, causing a little tickle.

As it became darker, the raft slowed down like a lazy mud turtle. Misty rays of light pierced the trees' canopy like flaming arrows. The current wound around little islands of ferns, moss, and fallen logs. This boggy swamp was indeed a silent and peaceful place. He wondered where the outlet was to the faster-moving river.

Was he alone?

*   *   *

He was not!

Two black bear cubs barreled toward him as if racing to see who could catch him first. Thankfully, they looked curious and playful, not like they wanted to chomp on him. Just like the beaver kits, the bear cubs just wanted to play with the raft. It must have been something they rarely saw on the river. They used their out-stretched paws to swat the edge of the raft. Back and forth they swatted. The calm waters soon turned into a torrent of waves like the lake's shoreline in a storm.

Mother Bear came to investigate the commotion. She silenced the cubs with a short grunt. She asked Wind Spirit if she could use the soap to wash her cubs. Wind Spirit granted her wish.

*   *   *

Delighted with the bar's lather, she scrubbed her cubs. Then she returned the soap to Windy with a big "Thank you."

He happily said, "You're welcome," then paddled into the main current and out of the swamp. But he realized his soap was slowly wearing away and was even more rounded on the edges.

"Ah," he said, "I'm finally back to the big river. I'm away from the young beavers and bears—and their mothers' wash."

*   *   *

Tired from his romp in the swamp, Windy managed a smile. He lay back and enjoyed the warm afternoon sun.

Later, he traveled between many fog-covered islands near the river's end. He was getting close to the big lake. He rode a gentle current to the rippling waves of the river's shoreline.

Surprised, he bumped up against an elevated nest. It held a bunch of eggs. As he looked inside, the mother swan returned to her nest and pounced on Windy. The swan beat Windy with her powerful wings again and again. Windy held the bar of soap tightly. She must have thought the soap was one of her eggs. Windy lowered his head and paddled away. She chased him and kept beating him with her wings. Windy held out the soap for her to see. She looked closely. Seeing her mistake, she smiled. Windy laughed, too, and wished her good luck with her young cygnets that were about to hatch.

Slightly wing-beaten, Windy paddled on. Misty fog grew so heavy it was hard to see.

*   *   *

Soon the current started going faster. Waves began breaking over the front of the raft. Windy thought he heard the wind picking up as he approached the big lake.

The raft gained more speed. That sound was not the wind; it was rushing water! Rapids roared, there was whitewater—dead ahead! Too late to portage around the rapids, he held on tightly. The front of the raft bobbed up and down in and out of the water.

Klunk! The raft slammed into a half-buried rock. Splinters flew as the raft spun around and turned over. Windy and the soap broke loose. He went one way, and the soap went another. After struggling and tumbling underwater, he suddenly surfaced near the bobbing soap—and grabbed it. With a heroic lunge, he exploded out of the water, grabbed the paddle, and climbed back onto the raft. He continued downstream, holding tightly to the damaged raft with one hand, cradling his soap with the other.

He finally found some quiet water and relaxed. The current carried them toward the big lake. A raven followed.

*   *   *

After drifting a while, Windy heard another rushing sound ahead. It sounded strange. He was concerned. Much to his surprise, the entire river was blocked by a fragile fish weir. It stretched across the water and directed the fish to a trap in its center. "Oh no!" he shouted. "Either I have to break through the sticks forming the funnel, or go to shore and portage around the weir."

The decision was quickly made for him. He crashed into the side of the funnel-shaped sticks and rode over the top of the weir.

The sticks sprung back to their original position. He moved on with only slight damage to the weir. He still had a firm grip on the soap!

*   *   *

As the river flowed into the lake, the water felt warmer. When the current slowed, he paddled toward the shore. He rubbed his eyes and watched for Raven Maiden. He hoped that she would be doing her wash today.

He found her! She was at the washing station. He paddled to her and smiled, keeping hidden his gift of soap.

*   *   *

When she saw Windy, she broke into a big smile, too. "You made it! I'm so excited! Come over here and clean up. You look like the river has tossed you around a bit. Come."

When he stepped off the raft, he dropped the soap in the water. His gift being discovered, he handed her the soap.

She said, "Oh, that's just what I need. I've run out of soap while washing my family's clothes. It looks like this soap has been on a long voyage, too!"

She gave Wind Spirit a quick hug! He was indeed a happy fellow as he helped her finish washing the clothes, a task not normally done by a young brave.

Later, he sat with Raven Maiden on the beach. They thanked the Great Spirit for protecting him on the exciting journey down the river. Both realized the soap he had made was a sign, a symbol of Windy's desire to reunite with her.

A raven croaked and perched nearby.

*   *   *

Wind Spirit held Raven Maiden's hand as she showed him her village. He met their chief, Soaring Eagle. Everybody welcomed him and made him feel very comfortable.

Proud that he had completed his journey—his Quest—Windy joined Raven for a swim in the lake. Then they sat close on a log and watched the sun set across the lake.

Windy smiled, happy that Raven Maiden would always be his friend.

HUMAN FACTORS

An Essay

I believe we've all had a positive accidental experience in life. This story relates to how timing and age were lined up in a positive way for me. Having received my MS in Psychology from Eastern Michigan University in 1972, I moved on to the University of Michigan in 1973. My graduate advisor there, Dr. Pew, the head of the psych department, suggested I continue my studies by pursuing a mixed major in a doctoral program in Ergonomics and Industrial Engineering. The basis of his recommendations was due, in part, to my current position at the Bendix Aerospace Division as manager of the Human Factors Group. He felt my academic studies would complement the real life design, test, and evaluation aspects of my work at Bendix. Especially since the current project for NASA was in evaluating human factors design for astronaut operations on the lunar surface. I was so relieved to be accepted, I looked for white smoke to billow from the buildings chimney.

He set up a meeting with Dr. Sharp at Industrial Operations and Engineering (I O & E) on north campus who gave tentative approval of the mixed major. He suggested several introductory courses to kick off the program and meet staff and other candidates.

Here is where the first aspect of an accidental positive aspect of timing and age materialized—in this case, age. Let me explain.

I O & E had just received a contract from Michigan Dept. of Transportation (MDOT) to evaluate several highway signs that may not have a clear message in the wording and graphics. The contract's goal was to verify their concerns and recommend changes to optimize the sign's goal: information to the driver. That's where my age stood out. All other students in the program were under twenty-five and my age (36) provided for a more acceptable range of age for test subjects in the initial testing. Later on, once the test format was established, an even broader range, to 70 years old, would be evaluated. Dr. Pew teased me frequently as being his oldest student—ever—with me being "Way north of thirty."

The second aspect of a positive experience was the eye-opening pleasure of running into my nephew Dave at the department's coffee shop. Yes, I knew he was at U of M, but courses in mechanical engineering were taught mostly on the main campus. East and West Engine radiated in opposite directions from the famous arch, the must-experience entrance into the diag from the south. Now 20, he was taking electives at the I O & E, at G. G. Brown building where half of my classes met. Most of you can relate to my feelings in sharing life with the first and only nephew. His parents, Milt and Irene, gave birth to Dave in 1953 while living on the farm as I was in my last years of high school. Here is the joy of my life in the '50s that I nurtured with joy, 21 years later. What a joy—again. He paid me back well for all those treats of riding with me on my horse, Chico, or on the John Deere tractor, or feeding calves with a teat on a milk bucket. Yes, he loved the animals and followed me around the farm for several years. It was like having a little brother. How'd he pay me back? Easy. I'd crash at his pad at times, study together, and (get this) tutor me in higher math when his skills outweighed mine. This positive relationship continued throughout our lives.

I've always been puzzled by how, in the sweep of life, we end up where we do.

Dr. Sharp decided the Psych Dept. should take the lead in testing the validity of the existing signs to reaction times and proposing changes to improve the sign's information/instruction to the driver. I O & E would set up the facility for testing and sign modification, and Psych would conduct the tests.

This was a logical decision since the Psych building, on central campus, was an old elementary school, and the buildings on north campus were brand new and big enough to duplicate roadway conditions for the testing. You might say the Psych building would fit in the Downton Abby design, turn of the century: old. In fact, next door the abandoned University High School (in 1960) housed the Education Dept. *Waste not, want not* was the rule there.

The students in the Psych Dept. developed a test article that measured the time, in seconds, between the subject seeing the sign(s) and recorded what was the intended instruction of the sign. Because of the learned response in testing, there would be only four (4) cycles for each sign. First, four with the original (troublesome) sign, and then four with the changed/improved sign. Eight subjects from Engineering Dept. would be used initially. Later on, the sample population would include 100 varied male and female non-students with a trucking or normal driver's license in an age from 16 to 70. The resulting raw data would be analyzed and recommendations presented for review by the MDOT.

In preparation for the study, engineering students spent a few weeks on the white board to determine actual roadway measurements, before the test set up. They considered known physical conditions, such as distance from the driver's eye forward to the sign for the test, distance of the sign from the right side of the roadway, and height of the sign above the ground. Many variables would not be tested including the interference of rain, snow, and fog, or the speed of the vehicle; however, lighting would be varied.

All the parameters would be tested on site in the future, these tests had built in limitations to be sure, but would answer many of the questions for future optimization of road sign instructions.

Again, the goal of the testing was to provide to the driver the most effective use of the printed word and graphics while traveling at 50 to 70 mph. The layout started taking shape with a simulated seat, steering wheel, and dash. The sign was actual size with MDOT reflective paint located at 150 feet on a straightaway with accurate roadside measurements. A rheostat on existing light varied the illumination. Headlights were mounted in a typical location.

Once in place, the driver's seat/test subject would be shown the sign by flipping up the opaque glasses. At that time a monitor would measure the time in seconds that it took to identify the instructions the driver saw and gave an oral report.

Each subject evaluated four (4) signs in lighted and darkened driving conditions. As I mentioned earlier, the MDOT had identified 12 troublesome signs. MDOT had data that indicated drivers had a little more trouble interpreting the instructions while driving at allowed speeds.

We were split up into three groups (A, B, and C), each evaluating four signs. I was in Group B. But I'll be presenting the results of the most interesting sign in Group A for two reasons: I was a test subject in that group, and it had one of the most interesting signs—DEER CROSSING with GRAPHIC. Yep, you've all seen this one. In fact, all of you hope to see a deer—not hit one. As you know very well, deer/auto collisions cost drivers and insurance companies millions of dollars every year, especially in the fall when the hormone-loaded romantic buck chases his mate in the season we call *the rut*. At this time of the year, they cross highways in hot pursuit to breed, lying caution to the wind.

SIGN MODIFICATION TESTED

The existing DEER CROSSING words at 6 by 3 inches were located under a graphic of deer's full body in a jumping to the left position, (no we did not allow for the British roadways). Wording took one half of the sign, the remainder the body of the deer. After several options were evaluated the recommended change was fabricated as follows.

In the *change*, the DEER CROSSING words were enlarged to 10 by 5 inches in the bottom half of the sign and just the head—with antlers' graphic on the top half of the sign. As such, it was larger and spoke to the same visual feedback: it's a deer. The resulting bust was larger and it provided the same instructions to the driver: Look out, deer have been crossing here frequently.

The test was repeated for II Low Light Driving depicting dawn and dusk when deer frequently are active near roadways, followed by III Night Driving.

There was a lot of set up and testing for days, this data is a brief sample to show a portion of the multiple testing conditions, with up to 100 test subjects. I picked this one as one example since it was a sign that I believe is interesting. Plus, you can draw from it some conclusions.

They are:

- The new sign appears to provide quicker recognition of instructions to the driver.
- Older subjects do not react as fast as younger subjects (as per Pew's thoughts).
- Some females take longer to respond to the same instructions.

Okay, you're probably wondering what were some of the signs our group evaluated; you'll see they were not as interesting as DEER CROSSING. However, our signs were just as important. They included: YIELD RIGHT OF WAY, with graphic; CONSTRUCTION AHEAD, with graphic; STOP SIGN AHEAD, with graphic; and LANE CLOSED AHEAD, with graphic. See? Not as interesting, but we felt the improvements we made had just as much merit.

These are preliminary conclusions to be sure, but this data provides an example of how testing leads to some conclusions based on objective test results versus empirical data.

Thanks for following some of my memorable times at school. I have shown some of the details in testing, set up, recording various design concerns. Believe me, at times you wonder if we could evaluate more options. But, as we evaluated the hundredth subject, it appeared we had enough data to make very good recommendations to MDOT.

Most of our changes were accepted by the MDOT, and you can see those results the next time you drive the Interstate. Notice the DEER CROSSING signs and you'll see the changes; this is all thanks to students at the University of Michigan.

BEAR HUNT

An Essay

It all started while attending the Grand Rapids sport show in the
early 1980s. My son Ron and I were wandering around the exhib-
its, admiring various sporting equipment, when Rich Dickerson's
Canadian Bear Hunts booth caught our eye.

"Let's take a look," I casually mentioned to my son.

A man of few words, he said, "Sure."

While looking up at a huge black bear mounted in an attack

pose, Rick wandered over and explained the size, year, and location where the bear had been harvested. Assuming we were interested, he introduced himself as owner/guide and went on to explain the basic rules of a Canadian hunt, cost, time of year (spring & fall) and location. In the White River area north of Wawa, in Ontario, he explained the differences between the spring and fall hunt, and permits required for out-of-country hunters. Another option for busy people was his recent addition of a three-day hunt versus the standard five. For busy people it works out well and is less expensive. Rich noted that he also worked for the Canadian DNR, doing guide work, as a part time hobby. He mentioned that, due to the excessive number of bears in the Ontario habitat, the Canadian Government has been encouraging hunters to come to Canada with the goal of reducing the bear population.

Sharp in marketing ideas, he mentioned that he had a special father and son hunt, with blinds/stands close together for more security in the bush. He did not gloss over some of the more mundane aspects of hunting, saying we would also be involved in tending the baits near the stands/blinds—which can be messy. I was impressed with Rich and his operation—especially being an employee of the DNR. We thanked him for sharing his briefing and told him we'd be in touch.

On the way home, we chatted enough to make up our minds that the spring three-day hunt would fit our schedules, since Ron would be leaving for the Naval Academy in June.

Turning in that night, Ron spoke up and said, "Dad, I can pay for part of the hunt."

I assured him his mother and I could handle the cost.

Several days later, Rich's wife Joan handled the arrangements for our journey. She also reminded us of what we could not bring into Canada—since those items would only be confiscated. Items such as hand guns, alcohol, and excessive cash would not be allowed.

"And don't forget your mosquito netting," she reminded us.

Our Starcraft van headed north at 5 AM Sunday morning, loaded with cold pop, coffee, and sandwiches, for the 700-mile trip. The rifle sightings had been set from deer to bear. Approaching the Mackinac Bridge, we absorbed the beauty of the vista of the Straits and the scent of fresh water in the air.

I attempted to grab a few winks after leaving St Ignes, as Ron drove through the beautiful pine forest headed for the Soo. It made no sense, of course, but it felt as though we were in another country. I imagined Germany's Black Forest must have looked similar, like the forest of my great-great-great- grandfather Johann George Rettig.

Ron barked for me to wake up. "Foreign country ahead."

We declared our rifles and ammo and answered all their questions. The border guards gave us maps of Ontario and sent us on our way, wishing us great success with our hunt.

As we headed north, I had a strange but welcome feeling of escape from the norm—a freedom or new birth. Maybe it was the striking change in the landscape of the massive stone outcrops mixed in with the pine forest; or perhaps it had to do with the vast expanse of Lake Superior's undulating crucible. As a biologist by training, I couldn't help but see the forest about me as the green lungs for the Earth's toxic emissions.

We followed the highway that hugged Agawa Bay and headed north to Wawa. Joan had told us there would be no problem finding the turn-off, since a huge Canadian Goose marked the turn.

"There it is," Ron hollered. It must have been 50 feet long with a 100-foot wingspan.

We met up with Joe, who was helping Rich after Rich had been called away to assist on a poaching investigation. Joe showed us our three-paired blind/stand locations on the map. They were named Cree, Iroquois, and Tlingit, and mentioned we'd be going with him to refresh the bait near the blind/stands. Our first sojourn into the bush was to the first set of blinds—called Cree—which was to familiarize us with its layout, the firing lanes, roads, and clues on hunting bear. The routine for the next three days was to go with him each morning to check and refresh the bait, then back alone to hunt in the late afternoon.

Despite being just ten minutes removed from the van after a 12-hour trip, we were back in a vehicle and headed into the forest.

We turned on a two-track without changing speeds, as Joe silently headed into the bush to check whether the bait had been hit the previous night. After a 25-minute bumpy ride, he showed us our blinds and the fields-of-fire he'd hacked out of the bush.

Joe's warning spoke volumes: "Shoot fast and frequently. Expect a shot while running."

We made a quick visit to the store next door called Last Stop. We picked up supplies for cooking and good old carbs. Dave, the owner, seemed to know the routine for hunting and offered his boat and rods for fishing in the local lake behind the store. I accepted, and mentioned we were tired from the trip to the bush with Joe. 700 miles from Michigan is a long haul.

He understood. "See you later," he said.

After we washed up, we grabbed a bite and hit the sack. I believe we could have slept on those basalt outcrops in the forest.

Joe's rattling old Ford woke us in the morning. "Let's go," he said, chomping at the bit.

We traversed the same route as the previous night. Neither mine nor Ron's bait pile had been hit.

We headed back to the cabin and took up Dave's offer to fish in the little lake. As we pulled in plenty of pike, we learned from other fisherman that we were breaking the local law—we didn't have license to fish. I could see the headline now: Father leads son into life of crime.

Being the first time we'd been in the bush, we began preparing early in the afternoon at the set of stands called Cree. After climbing in our camo, we taped all joints: shoes/pants, sleeve/gloves, and shirt/pants. We'd use the mosquito netting once we reached the woods. Concentrated pine scent masked our human scent. If I missed a bear, I could always blame the netting.

We took off at four hoping to be in our stands by five. While dropping Ron off at his stand, a few natives stopped by on their way to fish in the lake. They asked too many questions about the van for my liking. Anyone could hotwire a vehicle and leave us stranded.

My stand was about 50 yards off the two-track, elevated about 20 feet. A permanent ladder leaned against the tree. As the sun kissed the horizon and darkness enveloped the forest, the no-see-ems exploded from wherever they stay during the daylight. I was glad for the netting.

I won't bore you with all my thoughts while trying to grow a bear on the bait pile, but my mind wandered from family to work to concern for Ron, and whether the van would still be there when we finished.

At nine I squinted at the pile as darkness prohibited a shot. I climbed down and felt lucky that the van was still there.

We doffed our clothes outside—a learned trick meant to keep no-see-ems out of your room. After sharing some of the day's events, we ate the last of our illegal pike and hit the sack.

Tuesday came with Joe's colorful truck rattling in the parking lot. We headed to the second set of stands, called Iroquois, and quickly refreshed the bait. They were further to the west, but still in the migration pattern of bear just coming out of their winter dens in the hill country.

Later, we drove directly from the bush to a local float plane hangar on White Lake, just north of our cabin. I had arranged earlier to give Ron a tour of the forest from the air. I had seen a

beautiful C-190 Cessna Radial on an earlier drive, and had scheduled a flight. It was exactly what I hoped for as I had Ron sit in
co-pilot's seat so he could feel the controls as we buzzed a few
animals and banked around the shores of Lake Superior.

We were back in the brush at 1700 hours, rearing to go to our
new positions on the outcrops. No Indians this time, but we did
run into some hunters going in to a different location. Tonight's
wind was not right. It was strong and at my back, which is not
good because bears can pick up a man's scent up to a mile upwind.

Supper was quick and within Canadian law: venison steaks
from Dave's freezer. Afterward, we went to bed, knowing this
was the last night of our trip.

Next morning, after settling with Dave, we packed up and
waited for Joe's truck. Heading east, Joe mentioned it looked like
a good day to hunt. There was no breeze, and a low pressure cell
brought in a drizzle. Good for us, bad for the bears.

At the Tlingit blinds, we refreshed the baits and began our
goodbyes to Joe—we'd not see him again if we didn't get a bear.

Ron had a good feeling, he said, as we headed back to the
cabin to get the van.

We explored Pukaskwa National Park along Lake Superior
that morning. We even took a quick dip into those frigid waters.
It was still and quiet when I dropped Ron off. As expected, a light
drizzle fell on us.

Ron's blind was open and on the ground—still, it was difficult
to get at the thing. Mine wasn't much easier.

I didn't expect to hear a report from Ron's gun, though I
strained at times convinced I'd heard a shot.

In truth, a bad day hunting is better than a good day at work.
And since it was getting too dark to see anything on my bait pile,
I called it quits. It ended up being a beautiful night; the lower
pressure cell had passed through, leaving a moist underfoot that

silenced walking. The stars and moon lighted the majestic branches of the forest as I drove toward Ron's blind. About 100 yards ahead I caught his silhouette in the headlights, which made me very happy.

Then it happened.

I saw the smile on his face and knew exactly what it meant. Well, it's possible that we'd have to find a shot bear lying in the bush somewhere, using only our flashlights to guide us.

Thankfully that wasn't the case. After a big hug, he told me the dead boar was all gutted and lay just over the rise, waiting for me to help carry it out. As a father, I couldn't have been happier.

We found the bear splayed out as if asleep on his stomach. We tied him to a large limb and stumbled out of the underbrush with Ron's prize. We also bagged the heart and liver, along with the various glands the Asians use for medical remedies. Our successful-hunt photo showed the bear draped over the spare tire of the van.

Curious, I asked about the shot and how it came about. Ron explained—with pride—that the bear came in on the right side of the field of fire. It was going to be a difficult shot at this angle, so he spun around while aiming his thirty-aught-six. The bear spotted him, and rather than run, the bear came at him with a brisk pace. Without the wind, the bear had no idea he was approaching a human. The scope's crosshairs zeroed in on the charging black furry mass. The round found the beast's heart and dropped him in his tracks—from just 10 yards away.

Rich skinned the bear, froze the meat, and Joe and Joan celebrated with us. We departed at midnight with our frozen hide and meat, and a proud father and grateful son winged our way south in our muddy Starcraft with stories to tell and experiences to savor for life.

A PERFECT WEEKEND

An Essay

In the spring of 1989, my daughter, Gay Lynn, in the Fine Arts Dance (ballet) Program at University of Utah, heard I was headed to Las Vegas for the annual Ski Show. Being so close to her in Salt Lake City, she invited me to come up after the show for a father and daughter weekend.

"That sounds like a plan," I said.

Part of the reason for me going to the Ski Show was indirectly the result of her attending the university—which had the best skiing in the States. Rather than her flying back after the winter holidays, we loaded up the van for skiing those majestic mountain ranges. I quickly discovered that five pair of loose skis inside the van was a real hazard. So, I designed a ski rack that mounted on the ladder on the van's rear door, with skis stowed vertically, making it a unique rack. Meaning, most racks mount on the roof of the vehicle. So, voila! The Ski Boot was born. It worked so well—it even had a plastic cover—I formed Redick Enterprises Incorporated (REI), applied for a patent, and started manufacturing the rack.

I had a booth the previous year at the Ski Show, and, in fact, had the whole family pulling booth time, to see if the market was there for my design. The booth had a mockup showing the rack on a van ladder, 4x4 rear wheel, and oodles of photos and handouts showing the mounted rack. As a part-time operation, REI sold a couple dozen racks as a satellite business for me.

This year I planned a moderate effort at the show by renting a van and mounting the Ski Boot on the rear ladder to demonstrate its use. As such, there I stood, next to the van, on the curb, as conventioneers passed by, going to and from the Hilton Hotel to the convention center. I felt like a barker in a carnival—not good, but I did manage a lot of traffic with little sales. A mistake, I pulled out early since I figured only one of fifty asked about the rack, and one of ten asked, "Why not have your booth inside?" They were right; a half-way marketing job was not working. Bolstering my spirits, two lovely ladies informed me that they had one of my racks—and they loved it. Let's see, that's two of five thousand attendants. I decided to install a more aggressive marketing plan the next year.

Anxious to get to Utah, I left the rack mounted on the rented van and departed Las Vegas that night. Then, believe it or not, I got some salve for my mental wounds. The manager of the Avis agency ran out to me as I was leaving, yelling, "Stop!"

"Holy smokes!" I said. "What's have I done now?"

Long story short: He wanted the rack mounted on the van and six more, as soon as possible. I told him that I could not sell him this one, but gave him my REI card and asked him to call the plant and we'd be delighted to sell him six at a good price. He was partially satisfied as I headed out toward Utah. To cheer him up, my last words to the manager, deadpanning Elwood Blues' checklist were: "I've a full tank of gas, a half pack of cigarettes, it's dark out, and I'm wearing sunglasses." That got a little smile out of him.

Stars faded from the predawn sky, and the moon winked from behind passing mountain peaks as I flew over the desert sands. Driving north through this arid land presented a few surprises as oodles of nocturnal animals pranced and slithered across the road in my headlights. Slow moving (squashed) armadillos, speedy jack rabbits, a sly fox, and leaping pronghorns in their beautiful tan, black, and white colors. It's cooler to travel and hunt at night while searching for a meal. Hard telling what other critters are lurking in the night. I hoped the van wouldn't break down.

The first hint of dawn painted a line of deep blue across the eastern horizon, erasing the faintest stars from the sky as I reached Salt Lake City.

After hugging and kissing, Gay Lynn and I ambled over to our favorite eatery, Charley's Place. Not sure if it was the visibility to the glass-enclosed flaming grill, the antique little white tile with black borders, old fashion stools (for those in a hurry), or the bread basket with every meal. Whether from the grassland, sea, or lake, you'd see your entrée sacrificed in flames on the grill as you ate your salad and crunched bread sticks.

Gay Lynn went over the itinerary for the next two days:

1. Climbing/hiking the Wasatch Range to the east this morning.
2. Horseback riding in the south during the afternoon.
3. Dinner down town at a friend's exclusive eatery tonight.
4. Skiing Sunday at Alta or Snowbird.

I said to myself, "Now there's a perfect weekend—if my body holds out. Climb, ride, ski."

Before I knew it, I was given a change of clothes, hiking boots, and we were headed up the Uinta Mountains on the Timpanogos Trail. When not in the blazing sun, we walked in the shade of Douglass Fir, Ponderosa Pine, Aspen, and periodically copse of Birch. I stopped and asked Gay Lynn to come over to the Birch trees so I could show her the tradition of us scouts while camping. Not having paper, our scoutmaster showed us how to find a downed tree or limb and peel off the bark to make a post card to send home. True, it was 41 years ago in 1948, but I can assure you the U. S. Post Office will deliver your card.

After having an excellent hike, several look-outs of interest caught my eye. Many were about the Ute Indians, and others about men who explored the area west of longitude 100, namely John Wesley Powell. I was surprised to find we had gone south enough to consider heading back when we reached Robert Redford's film colony and fine arts teaching center called Sundance. We ambled down, toured the grounds, got a cup of fresh coffee in the rustic lodge, found and acted in the outdoor theatre-in-the-round. With one person in the audience, I repeated some of the Shakespearean lines from my high school play performances. I brought the house down—so said Gay Lynn. Two other tourists also clapped with Gay Lynn. Not knowing when to quit, I launched into my falsetto and gave the audience of three Roy Orbison's "Oh Pretty Woman."

Gay Lynn said, "Time to move on."

My theatrical skills challenged, and my feelings hurt, we moved on to the chair lift on the ski hill as a way to get back to the trail, back to our van. Again, Gay Lynn impressed me as she moved; it was with the grace of a willow in the wind.

Back at the apartment, I met her roommate, took a quick nap, and we readied ourselves for the mustangs of Utah's southern range.

The stable was south of town, in the foothills of the mountains. The wranglers were expecting us, and we mounted and took off into the treeless, desert-like terrain with arroyos cutting across our path frequently. They'd been carved into the earth from a stream of water gone dry; we found ourselves riding in them rather than across. At one point, our guide, Wind Spirit, a Ute, mentioned that we could ride off alone, since we looked responsible. Riding toward the western horizon, the sun had just slipped behind the highest peaks, painting the entire range in a warm glow. A gentle breeze tousled Gay Lynn's hair as she galloped ahead of me. While watching her, Wind Spirit mentioned the insurance company covering this operation required a guide, after several frivolous suits.

"You know," he said. "It's a suing society in which we live."

I understood completely.

As Gay Lynn and I separated for a moment, sure enough, my horse stumbled in a depression. It was kind of the shape of a burial plot. Wind Spirit, always alert, saw my horse stumble and checked its hooves and leg. He appeared to be okay. Then I saw the little cross, the name Jimmy emblazoned on it. The cross may have caused the stumble.

Looking for a little humor, I said, "That's it. That's where Jimmy Hoffa is buried. We've finally found the place."

I figured the Indian would get the joke, but apparently not.

"What did you say to Wind Spirit?" Gay Lynn asked.

I told her of my joke.

Gay Lynn said, "Your joke failed. They think Hoffa is really out there. Wind Spirit told his friends to get shovels."

"In that case, let's get out of here."

Our dinner in town was as advertised: polished silver, linen tablecloths, and a extraordinary menu to tackle. This was quite a come-up from our eating with our fingers, and drinking—with cupped hands—out of a clear running creek while on the trail. I over ate, as I've been known to do. However, Gay Lynn's friend did his best to impress us—or was it her he meant to impress?

Then again, she made it clear he was not her boyfriend, just a friend who happened to be a boy.

I slept like a log Saturday night; I'd been going for 48 hours and needed some shut-eye.

As we passed the 5000-foot mark, we were grateful we did not have to stop at the turn-off to put chains on our tires. We passed Alta at 5000 feet and decided to go all the way up to Snowbird, whose summit is 12000 feet. That's seriously thin air up there.

Tow tickets paid, skis on, away we went on the chair-lift to check out our skills. It had been a while. I soon discovered Gay Lynn's parallel turn was smooth as silk, and her downward plunge an adagio, lifting and balancing as in a ballet. I guess I should have expected her skills. She's been living out here for two years in the best skiing area in the nation.

However, I do remember teaching her how to ski at Mt. Brighton in Michigan at age 6, back in the early 1970s. Her last 25 years as a balletomane showed itself as she glided down the hill ahead of me. I didn't ski so smoothly; I had a few rough edges.

It was time to try the big one, so we took the gondola to the summit. Expecting to see for miles from the top, we were shocked. We could only see the top of clouds. Over the last few hours the entire mountain had been enveloped with stratus clouds from 1000 to 8000 feet. Don't get me wrong, it was beautiful, but like flying in an airplane in the clouds.

I had an idea I could take her in the slalom, so I found the hill with the gates set up and the challenge was on. Down we went. She beat me by 10 seconds. I claimed a penalty on her time because of the age difference. She was having none of that. Experience, she said, is the equalizer.

What a day. I had one more competitive shot at her.

"Race you to the bottom," I said.

I should have saved my breath. She was waiting for me at the check-out. Oh well.

Our drive to town was noisy with talk; the drive to the airport was quiet.

Alone on the trip home, I had time to reflect on the honor in being a father, the honor of having a fine daughter (and other children, too). I relived every moment from the previous 48 hours.

As I looked back at the mountains from the plane, the area seemed to me as a chrysalis. I had changed over the beautiful weekend, not unlike the change the stunning Monarch Butterfly experiences during its metamorphosis.

"Thanks, Babe," I said to myself. "Let's do this again. How about every year?"

FISH ON

An Essay

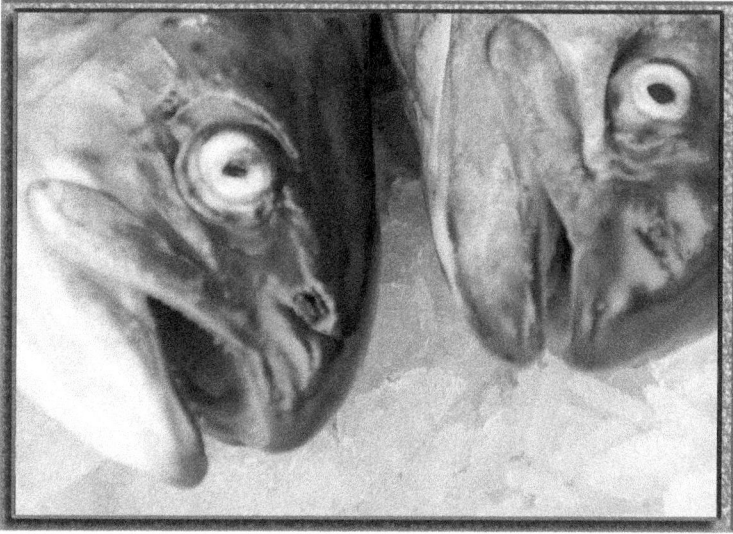

Fishing for the illusive salmon in Lake Michigan can frequently be a little more exciting than planned. This has certainly been true in my case, especially so in late summer when the mature fish start schooling at the mouths of various rivers that flow into the big lakes. There are Coho, Kings, Atlantic salmon, and Steelhead getting ready to spawn. Many boats start trolling above this mass of future fillets at the river's mouth; clever fisherman fish above the margin between silted river water and the clear water of the lake. The darker plume is visible to a trained eye of experience on the water; others may not see it. This is the area where the feeder fish hide as they dart in and out of this natural hiding place. And logically, this is where hungry salmon lurk. It is not unlike a feeding frenzy since once they start their spawning run up the river, they no longer feed. They have one goal in mind: reproduction. Not

just anywhere, either; only in the headwaters where they origi-
nated. Yep, either by smell of the water, temperature, its contents,
or turbidity, the salmon returns to its place of birth.

The female prepares a simple bed in the stream's bottom, re-
leases thousands of beautiful orange eggs called roe (caviar, if pro-
cessed) and the most aggressive male hovers over the bed
releasing sperm (called milt). Yes, many eggs drift downstream
unfertilized, and many are eaten by other fish. But as you know,
in nature's plan in propagating species, thousands are planned
knowing only hundreds will survive. This is a fatal run as both
will die on or near the spawning beds. By this time, they're ready.
Their bodies are beat-up from swimming against the current over
hazards, and are emaciated from not eating. No, if accidentally
caught, they would not be good eating.

There's an old saying that rings true to me: *You know you're a
true friend if invited to fish.* No one spends the day on the water with
someone he doesn't care for. I love fishing with friends and my
children, but in my case, it's my wife, my first mate, that heads the
list. She knows the boat, the equipment, and the fish. She also
knows when to have fun and when to get to work. My fishing
buddies, Hazen, Meston, Wagner, among others, say it well:
"Fishing does not count when measuring your time on Earth. It's
exempt."

Getting on with my story; how do you get those feeding fish
into the boat and onto the grill? Most of us use a variety of colors
on Spoons and J-plugs; these lure have a lot of action and come
in many colors. They range from bright red, glistening orange,
sunny yellow, lime green, blistering blue, cool indigo, and passion
violet. Yep. R-O-Y-G-B-I-V, the mnemonic you learned in science class; the colors of the rainbow.

That's enough background. Well, maybe not; one more item.
This is for readers who have not fished in the big lakes for salmon.
Many of us use downriggers which, on a cable, lower three pound

weight to the desired depth, with the line attached on a quick re-lease device. A typical boat has four downriggers on four rods spread out of the stern as the boat trolls at very low speed—1 to 1-½ knots. Got it? Can you picture the boat trolling near the mouth of the river, with others, with four rods reaching down 20 to 40 feet, dragging colorful lures about 30 feet back over a school of fish? Yep, it's a large swath of water. When highlining surface lures, it's even bigger. In this case, the lure is just below the sur-face, about 100 feet behind the boat.

Okay, enough background. Our boat, *Windward,* a 31 foot Ti-ara Slickcraft, has a typical layout with the added aid of a fish finder that tells us where the fish are located. It's a simple elec-tronic pulse, that if impacting a floating mass below our hull, usu-ally means fish. If nothing registers on the graph, the pulse hits the bottom and you know there aren't any fish in that area. As to what color to fish on any particular day, school's still out on that option. I've used yellow on cloudy days, sunny days, and rainy days, with equal success. Yet, charter boat captains, like Draper on Red Boat, will purposely start a little chatter on the marine radio, asking what color is catching fish. I believe, at times, he is just teasing the other boats on what's working. I believe the fish will hit on any color when they're feeding.

Okay, here's the perfect setup for me to fish: I'm at work, my first mate calls and says, "Let's go; by the look of the boats at the mouth, the fish are schooling, ready to spawn."

I reply, "See you at the boat."

My fellow friends at work know where I'm going, and the sec-retary knows how to contact me on the marine radio or cell phone, so no matter what's going on at work, I'm gone.

First to the boat, my mate will drop the canvas, clear the spider webs (those with boats know what I mean), and set up snacks and drinks for the fight ahead. As soon as we clear the channel, the downriggers are mounted, lines let out, weights lowered, and we circle the pack at the mouth.

I have one eye on the fish finder, and the other on the pack as we jockey for position on the margins of the dirty/fresh water line. I've had time to drink most of the *fisherman special* (schnapps & whiskey), and with that I say, "Babe, I'm ready for some action."

She's feeling a little spunky and says, "For fish or for me?"

Unable to choose such an offer, I say, "Both!" I grab her waist, get a hug, and we both watch the pack, the finder, and the bobbing of the rods.

Our neighbor, Scheuerle, in his boat, *Fire Drill*, passes by and gives a high sign as we weave through the pack with him on our starboard. Draper's red boat is on our port looking like a spider with at least 6 lines out. Yep, it's crowded.

"Say, my Mate, we're at the right depth," I said, "on the margin and going 1.5 knots."

She must have seen something in the bob of one of the poles on the port side. She slid from my side, took it out of the holder, and held it fast. Sure enough, the tip of the rod popped up and bent down.

She yelled, "Fish on!" Then she went about her business of setting the hook and adjusting the line drag so as not to let the fish break the line with a sudden run. Likewise, she began reeling in her fish in a controlled yet aggressive manner.

"Looking good, babe," I said. "Looks like a big one."

I was moving to steer the boat and clear the other rods and downriggers so the fish would not wrap itself in other lines or cables. Then it happened.

On the starboard, one of the rods not only had the line released from the weight, the rod was already bent over like a crescent moon, bobbing up and down feverishly.

"Fish on!" I yelled, "—a double."

"What the heck!" she exclaimed.

I hustled around the stern bringing up downriggers, reeling in rods number two and three, while number one remained in its holder. All I could hear was *wwwrrr* as the fish ran away from the boat. I put two inactive rods in their stowed rack and jumped back on number one with the drag still singing at 300 of the full 350 feet of line let out. Luckily, the line had not snapped. As I cleared the deck, my first mate was kind of silent—as though in trouble.

I was right.

"We have a problem," she said. "The fish is running back to the boat and I can't keep the line tight."

"Hang tight," I told her. "I'll turn the boat."

No sooner had I said so, I discovered boats on either side. We had no room to maneuver. "You'll have to walk along the gunnels to the bow," I explained. "Just don't go overboard."

As she stepped up on the gunnel and moved forward, she felt another problem. A J-Plug on a rod in the rack caught on her shirt and held fast. As she moved toward the bow, her shirt began to tear.

I grabbed the line cutters and went to work. The next sound I heard was a loud *zing!*

I ducked as a J-Plug lure flew over my head with a ragged piece of cloth hanging off the hooks.

She retreated to where I was, with her hot new racy look—with an altered shirt! After a short battle, we managed to land a nice 16 pounder—a true beauty, for sure.

We turned our attentions to the fish parked on rod number one; with a net we secured the second fish, and sure enough, we had a *double* under trying conditions.

Suddenly, the edge of the pack that had witnessed the fight blew their horns in celebration with us.

With the fish in the cooler, *Windward* headed into port, and we relaxed with our well-earned fisherman's specials. It had been a great day on the lake.

"I'm seeing a little more with your new lure-styled shirt," I said. "I kinda like it."

"Stop it," she ordered. "You've already seen all that's there. But at least your buddies didn't get a look."

"Not so fast, my dear. A couple of boats had their binoculars on you."

"Why am I not surprised?"

THE MONARCH

An Essay

I'd like to share with you a few of the rewarding experiences with the best known of the migrating butterflies, the Monarch (Order: Lepidoptera; Family: Danaus Plexippus). Okay, I know your science teacher at one time told you more than you felt you needed to know, but give me a chance to relate some unique experiences I've had—you may find them interesting.

Of the 112,000 different kinds of moths and butterflies in the world, about 11,000 are in North America. The number of monarchs vary from year to year, but it's estimated their numbers range from 50 to 500 million, depending on mortality rates. That's a staggering difference by any measure; later I'll discuss the reason for this variance.

Our subject is very easy to identify from its relatives largely due to its coloration. If you examine this complex color pattern on its wings with a small magnifying glasss, you'd discover the beautiful black and orange color is formed from thousands of tiny scales in a geometric arrangement. Its beauty has earned place at the top of the Lepidoptera world frequently called its reigning queen.

My interests started about twenty years ago when this multi-generational migrant appeared in my garden, dancing around its favorite red flowers. At the time I was unaware its dance, fluttering from flower to flower, was not only to drink in the sweet nectar, it was also looking for milkweed plants. Why? The milkweed is the sole source of nourishment for its offspring. Luckily I had several. Offspring? Yes, but much more than offspring. You see, when the female lays its egg(s) on the underside of the milkweed leaf, it does so since the hatching offspring survives *only* if it has access to the milky sap of the plant.

Let's clarify what we mean by offspring. Yep, you knew it was coming because your former teacher had you memorize the four steps in complete Metamorphosis: *Egg* to *Larva* (caterpillar) to *pupa* (chrysalis/cocoon) to *Adult*. Did you remember? I'll bet 90% of you did. Why? Because when your teacher presented reproduction in the animal kingdom, s/he must have mentioned that the multigenerational migrant monarch's complete metamorphosis is one of the most complex reproductive cycles in nature.

Yes, even more complex than your intense interest in Mary Sue in the 10th grade—the one you later married and completed your own kind of metamorphosis years later, sans milkweed.

Our monarch female, identified by a slightly different scale/color pattern, is a different story of intense activity to breed since life is measured in months, not years. Plus, she *must* find a milkweed plant on which to deposit her eggs. If she fails, the cycle comes to a screeching halt, and she dies.

Do you feel the segue to the most important part of this cycle? Yes. It's the milkweed plant. So if you choose to help the orange icon succeed in its reproductive cycle, work on saving the plant from wanton chemical destruction and cast as many milkweed seeds as you can from its protective pod. Then let nature take its course. You'll love the little parachutes each seed has as you cast it into the wind. Don't worry; it will find a low spot and germinate. Having the bulb type root, this perennial will not only come up every year, it will also expand itself into a little colony. Of course, you can also dig up the bulbous roots and transplant the plant into your garden or flower beds for they're very hardy and take the shock of transplanting very well. As for me, I'd rather distribute the dried seed in the pod to friends and have them cast the seeds in the wind—it gives others a good feeling. A word of warning, the milkweed in question is called the Swamp Milkweed, not the Tropical Milkweed (asclepias curassvica) which does not die in the winter, there by confusing the monarch's migrating patterns in Canada.

It's time now for me to present a simple outline of the complex 3,000-mile migrating pattern north across North America and return to Mexico. The adults are bunched together for about 6 months in winter hibernation in the forested mountains of the eastern coastal range near Nevolcanic, Mexico. In the spring they leave the bunched group on the tree limbs, mate, and fly north in what we call the Central Flyway.

Traveling about 50 miles a day, depending on weather conditions, the female generally reaches Texas or Arizona in 15 to 20 days. While feeding on nectar in the area, she looks for a milkweed plant on which to lay her egg(s). After doing so, she continues feeding until her death. (A few monarchs also fly up the coast of California in what we call the Western Flyway). After the egg hatches and the caterpillar grows, it morphs into a chrysalis, and a new adult monarch appears (complete metamorphosis). Then the *1st Generation* female mates, gains strength locally, and flies north up the center of the States to about Kansas or Missouri.

Upon arrival, she feeds on nectar while seeking a milkweed plant on which to lay her egg(s), and once again the mystery of complete metamorphosis takes place and the *2nd Generation* emerges. Then the female mates and flies north to about Wisconsin or Minnesota. At this point, some of the monarchs broaden their flight pattern and fly northwest up the Ohio River Valley into the Great Lakes States and, at times, all the way to a few New England States.

Again, after feeding and finding a milkweed plant, the cycle is repeated as the mystery continues producing the *3rd Generation*, the female mates and flies across the Canadian Border.

At this point a radical change in the breeding cycle occurs. The 3rd generation feeds until frost kills all the plants, and this 3rd generation reverses course and flies south to Mexico, its origin. Yep, an entire generation (great-grandchildren) turns 180 degrees and finds its way to its wintering grounds in Mexico.

I think it's amazing!

Yes, some do not make it, and others that do are beat up. But the majority do arrive to hibernate during the winter months up north. How do they know to fly south? One thing is for sure, there's nothing but dead plants in Canada. Chemical markers along the way? You tell me.

Now that you have the background on the mysterious life cycle of this orange icon, let me explain how I got involved in its life.

Back to my garden and the dancing Lepidopteras.

In June I discovered a monarch caterpillar with its bright yellow, white, and black stripes at the base of a milkweed plant in my garden. I duly returned it to the leaf so it could continue feeding. Right move? Wrong. The next day it was gone. I swore the next one was going into a bag in my room.

I soon learned there are many predators that feed on succulent grubs and caterpillars in the garden. These include: the Baltimore

Oriole and its cousins, Assassin bugs, spiders, flies, wasps, and many genera of ants. Stung once, I would not to be stung again when I found another monarch caterpillar. I took it inside in a clear bag with a whole milkweed plant. This was one of the most interesting scenes in the room—certainly better than the TV or my bulletin board photos. The little guy ate noisily 24/7 and within a week had doubled in size.

Then it happened.

It spun a filament to the leaf to hang on, curled up on itself, and spun a beautiful green chrysalis in just a few hours. Now, that was amazing to watch. Not to be outdone by that act, three days later the green case turned black and orange and within hours a stunning monarch emerged. That was the first time in my life I had witnessed what I'd seen in photos over the years.

Another dramatic aspect of its emergence was the unfolding of its wet wings in a jerking movement—not unlike a F-18 Hornet fighter plane. With a measured beat, it flapped its wings as if to try them out and dry them out.

Yep, I ran out of the room and showed everyone who would look at my new monarch before letting it go. Some, I'm sure, compared me to an expectant father showing off the new offspring. But to me, I was just blessed to see Mother Nature up close and personal.

Most are vagabonds; when you see them in the garden, they are on their way to somewhere else. Your garden may be a rest stop on the butterfly freeway, a place where they could linger a while, enjoy food, water, and shelter—and perhaps leave their eggs in payment. Be on the lookout.

Will you be able to see this mystery? I think so—or maybe not. If not, you are more likely to see them feeding on nectar or gathering in puddle clubs as they often gather in areas of nutrient-rich soil to suck up the mineral broth. They also love manure tea, for they are not only after the moisture but the dissolved salts and sugars.

Although illegal deforestation and severe weather contribute to their decline, recent research suggests that the biggest culprit are farmers' large-scale use of herbicides in their fields that also destroy milkweed next door. Monarchs need to feed on the plant—but it has decreased 21 percent in the last 15 years. That does not bode well for the butterflies, whose life span is so short. Remember, those making the next migration will be the great-grandchildren of the previous migrators.

This tragic opera isn't over. The worst is yet to come in the form of increased worldwide air and water pollution, which can be more destructive to the delicate systems of birds and butter-flies than to humans. Enough said.

Finally, I'd like to thank the 2015 Monarch Survey Team of family and friends for their work in recording monarch activity from coast to coast. They are: Don, in California; Madeline, in Arizona; GayLynn, in Utah; Tom, in Missouri; Ron, in Michigan; And LeAnne, in Virginia. As expected, with Tom and Ron being in the center of the Central Flyway, they had more sightings and observed several monarchs going through metamorphosis. Like-wise, not unexpected, Madeline, in Arizona, recorded sighting the very first monarch in the survey in April.

*   *   *

For a good novel about the monarch's plight, grab a copy of *Flight Behavior* by Barbara Kingsolver.

STEAM AND TEAM POWER

An Essay

As with many memorable experiences in our youth, later on in life we look back, in part, to relive these life-changing events. As a teenager in the early '50s, I was unaware of the privilege I had to work on the farm using technology of the 1800s. This opportunity presented itself through my Uncle Del, who built and collected steam engines and harvesting equipment that were the backbone of farming at the turn of the century. Being a typical teen, my interest before moving to the farm, at thirteen years of age, was focused on sports, cars, and girls.

Then, on the farm, Del's steam engines caught my attention. As such, I will share the various applications of the 1800s steam power used on our farm in the '50s. I'll concentrate on threshing corn with steam power, which involved learning to drive a team. This activity had such an impact on my life, I'll share it with you, too, and to a lesser extent, the additional joys of filling the silo with steam; lifting and rolling loose hay into the barn loft; and pulling stumps in the back forty. All of these were some of the experiences that affected my life as a young boy.

I'll start with threshing corn shocks that had to be retrieved from a wet field with a team of horses. Corn shocks? Yep. In the 1800s a binder would cut, bind and set aside corn stalks together in shocks to cure and dry in the field. When the ear of corn was dry and ready to separate from the cob, the shocks were brought to the barn, where the corn thresher separated the cob from the stalk, the kernels from the cob, and chopped the stalk fine enough to blow into a pile or, preferably, to the barn as with hay. The resulting fodder was used for both bedding and feed.

Lucky for us, one day our neighbor, Old Pistol Pete, who still had a team, told us we could have the remaining shocks of corn in a field too wet for retrieval with a tractor. He knew of Del's hobby with steam, and that he had a corn thresher. There was, however, one catch in the deal: the field was so wet he was certain we'd have to use his team.

You guessed it. Dad and Del jumped at the chance, and within hours, we were at Pete's barn where he showed us his prized pair of Belgians: their names were Jake and Jack. With massive shoulders, neck, and huge rump, their appearance, indeed, represented the term horsepower very well.

Pete commented, "Since your dad wanted you to learn how to harness a team, let me give you some advice before we start. I want you to talk to them as though they were your good old friends, pat them and talk with them frequently, so that they know who you are and get used to your voice. Also, speak in a crisp clear way so they know you mean business. And, by the way, keep your feet from under theirs. They won't know if they've stepped on yours but you damn sure will."

With me being only five feet tall, Dad slid a chair to me as Pete led the horses to the edge of the corral. *Dang, they're big,* I thought, *and those hooves are big as pie tins.*

My look at Dad clearly said: Am I going to be able to do this? He sensed my doubt, and said, with his eyes and a nod, *Go for it, Son.*

"Let's start with Jake. Here's the two-part collar, the first is a pad, the second, the leather collar that the traces are attached. Go ahead, get on the chair and give it a go." (Yes, he was British.) I reached around and while hugging Jake, I slipped on the collars. Pete helped me kind of throw the harness over Jake's back and secure it with the belly and back straps. Then, we buckled it to the collar, a very uncomfortable experience, being under the thousand-pound animal.

"Please don't move," I said to myself.

Giggling, Pete said, "Don't forget the crupper."

"The what?"

"The loop that you pass the tail through to keep the harness from moving forward."

"I'm to thread his huge tail through that little loop?"

"Sure," he laughed.

"I don't think Jake will like that, huh?" I said.

"Yeah, you're probably right. Okay. I tease. It has a buckle to open it, to help loop it around his tail."

I thought, as soon as I handled his tail near his butt, he'll look around which was enough to scare the bejesus out of me. I imagined him thinking, *Stay away from my private parts.* But, as I did so, there was no problem. I just told him what I was doing, in a crisp way, and he looked back briefly and then faced forward. Thank goodness. The bridle was last. Lucky for me he took the bit without a problem as I slid it over his ears, buckled it tight and routed the reins through the terret rings.

Finally, I routed the traces through the harness loops and laid them on his back.

"Good job, Son. Let's get Jack harnessed. Daylight is a bumin."

"Oh no," I said to myself, "a British John Wayne."

Jack was as docile as Jake, and with all this experience—one horse—it went a little better and faster. I loved it. Jack was a little more active with his feet, and I had to move several times to avoid losing a foot. I believe he was a little more restless just because he was anxious to team up with Jake, and work.

Pete moved in and tied the team together, attached the reins, and asked me to fasten the traces to the whiffletree. He moved the duo to the wagon, attached the tree to the wagon's tongue, and handed the lines to Dad.

"You're ready to go, fellows. Away with you."

Finally, we were in business. Dad let me drive the team once we got to the cornfield.

Giving them their lead, we moved cautiously along the intermittent shadows and dappled sunlight of the afternoon along the corn shocks. I felt like a million bucks, with lines in hand, I was in charge of a couple thousand pounds of powerful horse flesh prancing along the field. I could tell they enjoyed working under harness. I just knew. Dad mentioned one reason for their smooth gait and classic movement was due to their matched size they naturally stepped together.

He added, "I'll bet, when they are pulling a heavy load, they also pull together, which is very important for maximum thrust."

"You're right, Dad, they seem to move as one. Pete must know they're a great team, and we're fortunate that he let us use them."

"Sadly, in another few years there won't be any teams left; so it's true, we're very fortunate, son."

"Oops! Hold on, boys!" I yelled as the team bolted and stopped. "What was that?"

Dad added, "That shimmering flash must have been heat

lightning that caught your team by surprise. Tell your boys what your mom used to say: God must be taking pictures."

Fully loaded now, we headed down the lane to the barn with a nice load. A load Dad put together alone, as he jumped on and off the wagon for a good hour. Pete was waiting for us as we pulled up to the barn. He unhitched the team, led the horses to water, removed their bridles, gave them each a feed bag and asked me if I'd like to help him remove the harness. I said to myself, "Is the pope Catholic?"

"Yeah, sure would, Pete." As we removed the harness I thanked him for the opportunity and likewise chatted with the horses. Sadly, I would most likely never see or drive them again. Just after hooking our John Deere to the wagon full of corn shocks, for reasons I alone could understand, I hugged each horse—and Pete, too. Dad knew of my actions, my feelings. Pete was in his 80s and not feeling that well, and I may never see him again—ever.

By the time we arrived back at our farm, Del had the steam engine ready to go, and he had hooked it up with a massive belt from, the engine's flywheel to the threshing machine. He announced our arrival with a long whistle. Within minutes we were, throwing shocks into the thresher's hopper. Cobs started flying out of the chute onto a pile. Shelled corn was being collected in feed sacks from another chute. The massive tubular arm was blowing chopped corn stalks into the mow of the barn; we were in business! In the middle of all this, I had to move my horse, Chico, from his stall, and release him in the barnyard.

He wanted no part of this activity. Mom was also busy putting the chickens into the coop, they, too, wanted nothing to do with the noise of the thresher or the engine's whistle.

Yes, this was a major event in my life, whether working with the team or threshing corn the old fashion way. I was a very lucky guy.

Part of the feeling was witnessing the change in the sound of the steam engine as it labored under a load. The slower rpm sound of *wump. . . wump. . . wump* was music to our ears as the governor kicked in. It gave the piston more steam and the sound changed to *wump wump wump*, as the rpm's increased. It was much like enjoying a team pulling steady on a heavy load. The sound was different but the same.

As many might say, you had to be in the thick of things. You had to be there to be able to feel its power in order to embrace the moment. That, I had done with the team and the steam.

As we continued to toil away, Mom approached the wagon.

"What did you say, Mom?" I said as she brought glasses of ginger beer to us old-timers.

She repeated, "Did you see the crowd that has collected along the roadside?"

I looked, and sure enough, a dozen cars had stopped to witness this 1800s event. Del must have seen them too and motioned to them to come into the yard and see the threshing up close—including chopped fodder on their clothes. One old timer even asked if he could feed shocks to the hopper.

"Of course," Del said. He knew it would make his day, we thought so, too.

Yes, Del taught me how to clean tubes on the engine's boiler, and make steam on his engine many times. But driving the team and loading the corn thresher with Pete, Del, and Dad, was one of the highlights of my life. I'm very thankful to have been asked to be part of history.

FLY AWAY WITH ME

An Essay

In the 1960s, the tradition of children visiting their parents' work-place crossed my threshold. It sounded like a good idea to me. At seven, my oldest, LeAnne, jumped at the idea of spending the day at work and smiled with glee when she heard of the bonus of lunch. Later that day, I overheard Lee asking her mother what she should wear: Dress or slacks? Can I wear tennis shoes? Grinning, I thought of how some things never change with females—no matter how young.

Things then changed as I learned a test flight in Ohio was scheduled for the day Lee had selected to visit. No problem, I thought. I'll take her along. It was to Wright-Patterson Air Force Base (WPAFB), in Ohio—which included NASA's Flight Operations Group. This would be Lee's first plane ride, mingling with my NASA and Air Force colleagues, an overnighter, plus a first time away from her mom. Again, she had no problem with our change of plans. However, she did have a passel of new questions. At her age, I expected as much. Yes, she'd meet an astronaut; yes, we'd stay in a motel; no, we would not have a meal on the plane, just peanuts and sodas.

Let me explain my job and how cool our trip could be for LeAnne.

While working at Bendix Aerospace (Bx) in Ann Arbor, I had the fortune of being selected to complete astronaut training (minus geology/flight). This happened because Bendix was designing and fabricating for NASA the Apollo Lunar Experiments to be deployed on the moon. As test and evaluation engineer in the Crew Systems/Human Factors Group, I was responsible for evaluating all the deployment tasks on Bx experiments the crew was to complete on the lunar surface. Our group was faced with many variables: 1/6 gravity, restricted movement in the Apollo Blk II space suit, collimated light, and many more. One design parameter was critical: never ask the crew to reach or bend over 45 degrees or he'll certainly fall over and damage the suit or the experiment. That was part of my job, to suit up and evaluate certain critical tasks. If, while testing at Bx, I found the task marginal or dangerous, we'd do further evaluation in the MSC water tank, or in the G-Force One aircraft at Wright Field. That explains our need to fly to WPAFB in Ohio. We needed to evaluate a questionable new design.

NASA's G-Force One was a modified Boeing 707 configuration as a KC-135—or a *tanker* in military terminology. It flew a series of parabolas over a large restricted area above WPAFB. Simulated 1/6 G or Zero G was achieved by climbing from 10K feet to 25K and then descending at various rates to simulate weightlessness in either mode. When suited, crew members would stand with you and provide support during these constant pull-out maneuvers. The G forces were so stressful on the body, the plane earned the nickname Vomit Comet.

Test personnel for this flight were all old-timers, including astronaut Don Lind, who was very familiar with Bx experiments. As such, I decided not to fly before leaving Ann Arbor. Don and I had flown together several times, and on this particular test flight, the Bx experiment evaluation was minor. We were just evaluating a new set of leveling legs.

It may sound simple to level an experiment, but remember, we did not know the surface conditions and the crew was leveling the unit at the end of a 24 inch handling tool. All of the instruments deployed on the moon had to be level to within +/- two degrees. This feature ensured equal thermal loading at lunar sunrise, lunar moon, and lunar sunset. This involved a temperature swing from minus 200 to plus 240 degrees Fahrenheit. Not to worry, the Central Station had a thermal electric generator (RTG) to heat the experiments at lunar night and layers of golden Mylar to reflect the sun at lunar noon.

At seven, everything was pretty much a new experience to LeAnne, as we checked our baggage and boarded the plane. We chatted about airplanes before taking off for Ohio. We were on one of the most reliable aircraft made—a DC-3. A classic; so sound in design and operation. Many critical short-haul flights are in the *Gooney Bird,* as it is often called. The plane takes off at 200 mph, cruises at 200 mph, and lands at, yep, you guessed it, 200 mph—hence the nickname. I noticed, on entering the plane, there was a brass plate showing the date of manufacture, location, and number of updates to the fuselage and motors. This plane was built in 1937. Ha! The same year of my birth! We were both 32 years old. I hoped to be in as good of shape. LeAnne was keeping a little trip log while I chatted about aircraft, so I mentioned to her the military design for the DC-3 and C-47. Her eyes went wide at the telling of there being more than 400 C-47s participating in the June 6, 1944, D-Day landing in France during WWII.

The short flight of 250 miles at 10,000 feet gave LeAnne a chance to see the earth from a new perspective. After a Coke and peanuts, she whispered that she would like to check out the facilities, admitting coyly, "I just want to say I tinkled at ten thousand feet."

Landing was another eye opener for Lee as she saw the Air Force Museum planes from the air as a couple of fighter jets screamed past.

At Flight Ops, I debriefed Don on the objectives of the new leg leveling design on the Solar Wind experiment. It proved difficult to keep his attention, a he found Lee more interesting. I understood. Don was also married with kids. He was also about my same age. I was upset that Don was not selected for an Apollo flight, but later on, flew on a shuttle. Very religious, as was fellow astronaut Jim Irwin, we all had a good time teasing and pressing for humor during work. Don was always kidded about the difficulty he had ordering his Mormon Tea (no caffeine, please) in a restaurant. "What's that?" the waitress would ask with a puzzled look on her face. He'd just give up and drink water. We also gave him a hard time over having to wear what appeared to be long underwear. Mormon doctrine required him to do so when married in the Temple. And we'd kid Irwin, as well, for taking several trips to Mount Ararat in Turkey, searching for Noah's Ark. When late for a meeting, we'd say, "Where have you been? Looking for Noah's Ark again?" We respected each other, though. That's what made us a tight crew.

As the G-Force One took off for the test flight, we headed to the Air Force Museum. It had an outside static display as well as an indoor panorama of current and historic aircraft. It was my first visit. I loved it and hoped Lee would too. However, I did not expect her to tie in the older aircraft as compared to current models. What did impress her was the dog on a stick and an ice cream treat that occupied most of her attention. Just as we strolled out of the building an alarm sounded near the control tower.

We hurried outside to find several emergency vehicles heading toward runway 2E. I spotted the plane coming in on its final and quickly discovered why all the commotion. We were about to see one of the last X-70 supersonic aircraft. We heard it was being retired to the museum, after it was considered too expensive and no longer needed. I told Lee how lucky she was to see this event. I marveled at the craft's long skinny white nose, with canards, as it reached out from the massive wings and engine housings. It reminded me of a praying mantis. I felt sadness at seeing her retired.

Once all the excitement died down, we headed back to NASA Flt Ops to see how the test flight went. Always in a hurry to get back to their home base, the crew was quickly debriefed before they departed. Don gave Lee a big hug before he hurried off to his F-28 for a flight back to Texas.

Later on, I relaxed at the pool and munched on snacks as the sun eased beneath the horizon. The day had been long for a certain 7-year-old. Inside our room, on the double bed, I almost nodded off before I received a little poke and a whine from LeAnne.

"What's up?" I asked, looking at a gal with a long face.

She said, "We haven't had dinner yet."

She was right. It was about eight o'clock. I figured with all the nibbling we'd done all day, we'd be fine until breakfast. But that wasn't the case at all. The girl wanted a proper dinner—most likely a reminder from her mother.

We went to a cool spot called The Prop. Its propeller caught her eye while rotating in the twilight. We had a super meal then hit our double bed by nine.

While watching late TV, with no rules for early bedtime, my little girl's head rolled onto my shoulder with eyes closed. Asleep now, with a smile on her face, I hoped she had dreams of a great day. I know I sure did. She had covered a lot for a seven-year-old. And that's the way it was in 1969; we did it together, as I said, Fly Away With Me.

SOUTH TO FLORIDA IN 1864

An Essay

To honor my great-grandfather Wesley F. Redick's participation in the Civil War, my nephew, Tom Redick, and I have unearthed his outstanding service in his unit, The 75th Ohio Infantry Volunteers. Wesley joined in time to fight in the Second Bull Run and many other battles through the end of the war. Here is an account of his participation in the terrible Battle of Gainesville, 1864, which I call: "South to Florida in 1864."

With the crushing defeat in Florida, I'm even more amazed at Wesley's miraculous survival. Although wounded several times, it's like he had a magic charm in his rucksack. He returned home to his farm in Ohio in 1864, and died at age 75.

Yes, I've chosen a story to show what it's like to be part of the horrors of war.

The war had acquired a decidedly nasty edge as it rolled into its third year. The exuberance and sense of gamesmanship of earlier days ended, and the courage had crumbled in the face of harsh realities.

The War Between the States, as Georgians still call the Civil War, had persisted into its third year. The Union Army had encroached in the Western theater through Tennessee, and for Wesley's 75th had marched into the heart of the South.

The two opposing armies settled into their winter camps and began to ponder the coming spring and what desperate battles 1864 might bring. Winter camp during the Civil War gave relief from combat, and while the lessons of the mud march meant most campaigns could wait until after Easter, the winter camp was for many a deadly place. A 19th century camp kept men in hard shelters—ditches dug in the ground for some enlisted men. It is no surprise that in this unsanitary condition led to casualties and death from disease. Wise officers kept their men well fed and active in the winter months with incessant drilling and plenty of ham, beans, and steak.

Wesley and what was left of the 75th—after the attacks on the harbor in Charleston South Carolina, they were down to 86 men—set up their winter camp on Folly Island. The winter of 1863-1864 was a mild but wet one, and the men ate more crab, shrimp and fish than they cared to—what had started out as a treat began to taste more like possum-en-mud cooked whole on the fire.

Up in Washington, President Lincoln faced a tough election ahead, as McClellan finally revealed the opposition he had for the "great ape" and declared himself a presidential candidate.

Lincoln gave Grant the sole generalship of the Federal chain of command as Lieutenant General of all Union Armies—a post previously held only by George Washington during the American Revolution. The Union's new commander set his sights on Georgia and the City of Atlanta and told William Tecumseh Sherman to prepare for his epic March to the Sea.

As the western armies began their march into Georgia, on

February 22, 1864, the 75th was ordered to take trains down to Jacksonville, Fla. What was left of this noble regiment, which had differentiated itself from the "Damn Dutch" Germans of the 11th Corps, was now attached to the 1st Brigade, Florida, the Division under Adalbert Ames' district. With minimal training, they were mounted on horses.

As Wesley took his new horse for a quick canter, he noticed the absence of Captain Dilger's artillery. Captain Dilger and Pig had been sent to assist General Sherman, and would be honored in Official Records for artillery work in the 1864 Atlanta Campaign during which his battery fired the rounds near Atlanta that killed Lt. General Leonidas Polk, Sewanee's Fighting Bishop and cousin of President James Polk.

With their horses, the 75th's ability to forage and change camps improved, and they spent the first month teeing up a very tasty corned beef and cabbage meal, organized by the remaining Irishmen. With several barrels of ale and stout, they cooked and drank and honored that Irish saint as well as anyone could have expected.

April 28, 1864 - battle action near Jacksonville.

May 31-June 3 -Expedition from Jacksonville to Camp Milton

On August 17, 1864, Wesley and the 75th Ohio fought their last, and most disastrous battle, in Gainesville, FL. The 75th Ohio Mounted infantry was joined by two companies of the 4th Massachusetts Cavalry, and an artillery unit called Battery A, from the 3rd Rhode Island Heavy Artillery that had three cannons. Along their many marches, they had picked up a few Floridians loyal to the Union.

By the time they got to Gainesville after two days' march, 55 miles south from Baldwin, Florida, the horses were near death from the heat, and the men were not much better (particularly the unmounted infantry).

Wesley watered his horse and got a beer from a very angry

looking barmaid. He wondered if she'd spat in his beer, but he saw nothing floating and was too thirsty to care.

All the Union troops were tired from travelling in the August heat and no one slept very well, either. For lunch the next day, the quartermaster butchered several steers and made officers steak and potatoes and the enlisted men a delicious beef stew for lunch.

As Wesley finished up his lunch and went to check on his horse, he saw men, including officers, nodding off from that big meal in their exhausted, sleep-deprived state.

Wes brushed his horse and gave him a bag of oats, then walked out into the street and looked south. He saw a cloud of dust in the distance, and thought he saw a flash of a bayonet or officer's sword in the hot sun. He ran back to where the 75th was arrayed in various states of napping, and shouted, "Colonel Harris, I think the rebels are coming!"

A stubby little major with mutton chop whiskers strode out of the house where the Colonel had established his headquarters, and said, "We're just finishing our brandy, boy, what are you yelling about?" As major mutton chop was walking toward Wesley, a solid shot cannonball beheaded him, and Andrew the bugler and David the drummer, seeing it fly by, blew Reveille and drummed their attack calls.

Unfortunately, all the units were taken by surprise by this attack from the South.

They were not fully deployed when the Confederate attack began with round after round of exploding cannonballs and solid shot ripping through the town and the half-assembled line of sleepy Union men.

For two hours, the Union men fought as residents watched from houses above. While cavalry mounted are not usually a match for infantry, these men tied the horse and moved forward through the town, taking nearly 200 prisoners in the process.

Many a man had taken his sleepy soul into a corner of a shop or residential house, and they were rousted and captured, heading for the hellhole called Andersonville.

Wesley and the 75th fought bravely, but 28 lost their lives and five folks, including Wesley, were wounded.

Wesley's wound was caused by flying shrapnel from an artillery shell which gave him a glancing blow that tore off a large patch of hair and skin from the side of his head. He collapsed under a porch and parts of several men, and lay there unconscious.

When Col. Harris gave the order to retreat from Gainesville; the Confederates continued to close in on the disorganized Union columns. Union losses numbered 28 dead, 5 wounded, 86 missing or unaccounted for, 188 captured along with 260 horses and one of the three 12-pound howitzers.

In a resounding victory, won through surprise, the Confederates only lost five men and thirty-five wounded. They celebrated in the streets with captured cattle and local beer, and no one noticed Wesley, who was in a pile of lumber and dead bodies on the main street, mostly out of sight, and completely unconscious for most of the evening.

Wesley woke in the middle of the night and wondered where he was. The weight of the men and lumber atop him was troubling, but he had enough room to wriggle painfully out from the collapsed porch.

He surveyed the street in the moonlight - no sentries seemed to be watching the center of town.

Guess I played possum and stayed put till they all went to bed! he thought to himself.

It was a bright moonlit night and Wesley still had his rifle, but no horse. He stayed off the main street and walked North through an alley—he found a horse tied up near one house, and with some gentle words, he cut the rope with his bayonet and led the horse to forage.

At the edge of town, he saw two sentries—one asleep and the other staring out at the forest in the distance. Wesley crept up behind him and slit his throat and killed the other sentry with a bayonet thrust as he woke up.

When he got about 20 miles out of town, he found around 40 Union troops, including Colonel Harris, camped. He got past the sentry and hit the hay, exhausted and aching from his concussion. The next morning, fearing possible pursuit, they all fled back to Jacksonville on their horses. While he reported his column was destroyed by a large Confederate force of 600-800 men and three cannon, there were only around 175 rebels who did the dirty work on the streets of Gainesville.

It was the last time Wesley would have to take a life. He mustered out in October 1864, ready to head home.

BROTHER MILT

An Essay

My world came crashing down in 1953 when Dad's chest X-Ray revealed stage two lung cancer. Yes, he was a smoker. I was already a little conflicted with the everyday vagaries of emerging manhood and its expectations academically, growth hormones, and personality development. In the center of the bridge from childhood ways to newfound maturity, this news of Dad's poisoned lungs had a critical effect on moving across the bridge. Okay, it's normal to be concerned about the future as the last days of high school slip by, layered with a soaring romantic stimulus of girls (coming from a family of boys, I knew little about females). The question: How involved should I get to this exciting opportunity/stimulus? Let's face it, at this age, probably all of us wondered what to do about our romantic interests. Who do you talk to? Who do you consult with on the right and wrong options of these feelings?

Certainly not Dad. He was sick and drugged from massive doses of antibiotics and morphine. Mom was busy as a care giver on a 24/7 basis. She had her hands full. Where to turn?

That's why I turned to my big brother Milt. He became the father figure I needed.

There were others, to be sure, such as Joe Broome—Mom's dad, who was there for me in the summer (he wintered in Florida). He taught me many aspects of construction in both wood and masonry. He was a prince among men. A WWI veteran of the British Armed Forces, he had a story about the evils of war. There was uncle Del, a stationary engineer with many technical skills, who helped me with the more mundane aspects of power—including steam. Yep, he built and restored steam engines as a hobby—and he taught me those skills, too. Just ask yourself, how many 14-year-old boys could fire up a steam engine? I could.

Nevertheless, immature for my age, I needed more help than was available. I needed to develop personal skills on how to cope with this new environment without a father. Milt was there for me.

Although Milt would soon be leaving our home, we were very close. Brother Dave was an okay guy but only 17 months older. And as they say, too close for comfort—when discussing personal concerns. Besides, he'd be off to college in 1953. Also, my friend and minister, Wanzer Brunelle, remained in Allen Park after we moved to Willis—as did our friends and relatives.

This relationship with Milt started back in the 1940s with his emergence as our babysitter. I remember his threats with his belt, as we misbehaved, to keep me and Dave in line. Nevertheless, he remained one of my heroes.

Here are some reasons why.

In the late 1940s Milt took me to Lincoln High School in Lincoln Park (Allen Park did not have a high school) for track practice one morning. I watched him run, we went for a swim in the pool (a first for me) and showered with the team. Dang if I didn't notice that I was missing something—pubic hair. I read later, in an old Nursing Arts book (where I learned about female anatomy) that I was not short changed. It would be coming soon enough. Milt probably thought little of the day, but I really enjoyed hearing the chit-chat and smack talk with his friends.

Also, in the 1940s, our family revolved around the church and scouting. For that experience, I'll forever be grateful. Although not convinced of the existence of supernatural deities, I appreciated the instruction on how others believe—faith issues and the Golden Rule. Scouting dominated our summers since Dad was a scoutmaster, Dave and Milt scouts, Milt the lifeguard at camp, and Mom one of the cooks. Being a cub scout, this made me a tag-along.

Many a night, Milt and I would play ping pong in the church basement. Likewise, I'd wait for him as he practiced playing organ.

Life in the 1940s changed dramatically going into 1950. We moved to a farm south of Willis, near Ypsilanti. I can never thank my dad enough for that life-changing opportunity as we all worked together, making a marginal house livable, repairing outbuildings, getting fields ready for cultivation. New and used farm equipment was readied for planting and harvesting. I loved it.

Milt had moved on to college, so Dave and I were the mainstay in helping Dad, who still retained his job in Detroit until 1951.

I missed Milt's caring ways as I evolved to a know-it-all teen with multiple distractions, such as girls, sports, and TV—but I survived.

Years later, in 1953, Milt and Irene married and moved to the farm, in Broom's cottage. Irene's brother George and I ushered the wedding—me, wearing my first tuxedo. Another cool thing was enjoying their first son, David Milton, as we moved about the farm doing chores, which included introducing Dave to chickens, pigs, and cattle. I loved being an uncle.

Here are a few Milt-isms:

I'm washing my '46 Ford one afternoon in readiness of a big dance that night, when in drives Milt with his first new car. The spanking new '55 Ford looked great compared to the old '46 Plymouth he'd been driving for years. He parked by the house and said without hesitation, "Hey, take our car and we'll use yours. You've got a big dance, right?" I was floored. I accepted, noting the odometer had only 22 miles on it. Need I say more about his caring?

After Dad died in 1955 at age 49, Milt moved to Ann Arbor. Brother Dave was at University of Michigan, so Mom and I decided that I'd commute to Eastern Michigan University and run the farm until I graduated. Fortunately, Mom got a job at EMU.

We had some good years on the farm from 1955 to 1960, but sadly, we had to sell after I graduated and left for the service.

Sure enough, Milt and Irene showed up at the graduation, which included the pinning of gold lieutenant bars on my uniform at the ROTC commissioning ceremony.

The beat goes on. He was also my best man in 1960 as I married the love of my life, Shirley, and gave me a bachelor party as well. Historically known to be unable to handle drink or smoke, he passed out that night. But guess what? He was there.

Early years in the Army took me and Shirley to Fort Benning, GA, Fort Devens, MA, and Two Rock Ranch Station, CA. Milt moved from Ann Arbor to Holly, north of Detroit, and William-ston, south of Lansing. At each move, Joe Broome and I modified the house by adding an additional bedroom. Some thought Milt a Catholic, what with all those children. I said, "No. He's just an active Presbyterian."

Here's another caring aspect of Milt. In 1964, Shirl, Mom, and my daughter LeAnne (age 2), were driving east to pick me up from summer training at Fort Devens, MA. Our station wagon had a troublesome noise in the rear end. So, typical Milt, he said, "Take our car. I'll fix yours. It's too risky to drive that far." Yep, that's Milt. Absolutely no personal concern, only concern for others.

By now you're wondering, when will the story about Milt's personal sacrifices end. They don't. I'm just going to stop now and explain some of the feeble ways I tried to pay him back. Of course, our upbringing taught us that it was not necessary to pay back favors; most choose to help without parody. However, after we bought the lake house in 1962, we sure welcomed the family for fun in the sun. By 1965 I believe there were six kids in sleeping bags scattered around the house. We always had a good time in the surf and sand. Much of which they carried back home in their shorts.

Yes, Joe Broome and I added many a bedroom to the homes of Milt, the wandering civil engineer. But we did it as a labor of love—no repayment necessary.

Later in my life, when I needed help with some legal issue, he was there again. In fact, one time he called on the governor's staff to ensure I got a fair hearing on my grievances. Then, having custody of certain funds for future use, he bailed me out with needed dental work that I could not afford.

There, that's the last beat of that drum.

I appreciate you hanging with me as I pay tribute to my big brother Milt, with incidents of caring that effected my life. We all learn many lessons in this short time on Earth, and to have someone ease you into a less conflicted life is worth noting. I have, with Milt's support. From a know-it-all teen, to a husband, father, and uncle, I learned a lot from all those I've met.

Milt always remarked, "There's not a person you'll meet in life that you can't learn from; everyone has a skill. Pay attention to those who are helping you."

As the old mule skinner said while harnessing Old Gray: "There's no education in the second kick of a mule. . . pay attention.

MY DAD, FRANK

An Essay

Let's start with Milt's (he's rarely called Frank) lineage in 1525 by Johann Conrad Rettig (a name based on *radish grower*) near the Black Forest in Germany, followed by Johann George Reddick, 1725 (Germany/Pennsylvania), then Leonard Conrad Reddick, 1770, then Jacob Wesley Redick (Fredrick, MD), then Wesley Fletcher Reddick, 1839 (Hocking, Ohio), and finally his father, Charles A. Redick, 1882, and wife Maude Marquis de Sellum (Butler, Ohio).

At thirteen, Living in Damaeus, Ohio, both of his parents died of influenza in 1918 (a worldwide pandemic had killed over five million in the U. S.). Milt helped place his eight brothers and sisters with farming families, and county shelters prior to leaving Ohio in the early 1920s. It remains a mystery where Dad went after leaving Ohio. Some say he was headed to California.

In any case, several years later, while working on a truck farm in Monroe, Michigan, he met my grandparents, Emily and Joe Broome, along with their daughter Marjorie. He moved into their home in Ecorse, and worked for Joe as a carpenter.

Mom and Dad married in 1929 (even though Emily told us later Dad hadn't a "pot to pee in, nor a window to throw it out!") Yes, Em had a way with words. This one cracked me up. One evening at dinner, when brother Milt announced that he and Irene were having their sixth child, Emily said, "If I were Irene, I'd open the window and shut it on his wangerdo."

With Joe and Emily's help, Mom and Dad built a home in Allen Park, at 15004 Cleveland. Dad worked for J. L. Hudson Co. and started a family: Milton Duane, 1932; David, 1935; and Ronald Lee, 1937.

*   *   *

With the following brief background, I'll present a few stories that have left a strong impression on me from the 18-year period between 1937 and 1955. My goal is to share my dad's personality, wisdom, and caring nature toward his wife and family—showing his positive strengths after a very difficult start in life.

I'll show the relationship in two quite different life experiences that were, at the time, at opposite poles. Thirteen years in Allen Park, and five on the farm in Willis.

In Allen Park, my recall from 1944 to 1950 (ages 7 to 13 for me) most of our activities centered around the First Presbyterian Church two blocks down the road on Cleveland. Why? Well, for starters, Mom and Dad were charter members (1930) and it seemed as though everything in our lives related to the church (and our English cousins that lived in Ecorse). A reminder, Emily, Joe, and Mom came to America in 1920, after WWI. Em's four sisters followed along.

Dad was superintendent of Sunday school, a scout master of the church troop, and a handyman to Mr. Jenkins, the custodian. I spent many hours with him while painting, fixing, or simply setting up tables for various dinners in the recreation room. Likewise, Mom was very active in the ladies' circle that ran the kitchen and served for the various dinners at the church. I don't know how many times I'd come home from school and find a note: *At church. Be home at four. And don't even think of sampling the cookies in the jar. They're for church.* Sometimes there'd be an addition: *There are a few burnt offerings on the plate in the breadbox. You may eat those—but only two!*

I figured out much later, since we were not wealthy and were unable to pledge ten percent of our income, Mom and Dad gave three times that much in service to the church. Dad once said, "Service is the greater gift to God." During the seven years that I recalled, Dad's major recreation was small-game hunting with a good dog. We shared ownership, with our Uncle Bill, of an outstanding German shorthaired pointer named Fritz. Uncle Bill also worked at Hudson's. Dad had gun rules: a BB gun at ten, a 22 at twelve, and a shotgun at fourteen. As such, when I went with

Dad's hunting group, Uncle Bill and Uncle Delbert Reich, I ran with the dog to flush birds out of their hiding place—be it pheasant, quail, or woodcock. He also hunted with our family doctor, Dr. Lee Heilman. More on him, my namesake, later. Many nights were spent with Dad in the basement, skinning pheasants, removing #6 lead shot, and stroking Fritz, who was dead tired from flushing birds all day. His muzzle, paws, and scrotum were beet red from running through the prickly dried plants all day. Later on I was allowed to hunt with the group—and I even carried a gun. More on that experience as you read on.

With me a cub scout, Dave and Milt boy scouts, Dad scoutmaster, and Mom camp cook, we all went to boy scout camp named Wakanda, near Gaylord, for two weeks in July, and then to Lake Gogebic in the U. P. on another vacation or two. (You'll enjoy one of my essays herein on revisiting camp ten years later.) Again, I remind you, the scouting program was aligned with the church, and we also went on many outings with the youth group from church. Frequently we'd go with Pastor Wanzer Brunelle. Got it? If it wasn't with the church, all our other activities were with the English cousins who lived in Ecorse or Allen Park. I'll not go into the number of evening we sat around the radio in the 1940s and listened to Edward R. Murrow, from London, as he reported on the war in Europe. Thank goodness we could not receive Tokyo Rose and her negative broadcasts over the Pacific war zone. Sadly, as many of my cousins went off to war, one of my favorites, Joey Hargraeves, died when his Hellcat crashed on a training mission. Dad made it clear that, at Christmas, we were not to play "I'll Be Home for Christmas" when Joey's mother, Jose, visited. Joey taught me how to make balsa model airplanes. I looked up to him, and for the first time, I felt the loss of a friend.

*   *   *

Before Dad reached 25 years at Hudson's, he apparently grew

restless for his lifetime goal to return to farming—his first love. In 1949 we spent many Sundays, sometimes with Em and Joe, searching for that long sought after acreage within our price range. After finding farms in Port Huron, Romeo, and Willis, with the help of Em and Joe, we bought 80 acres in Willis for ten grand. We moved to those 80 beautiful acres that spring, to a house needing plumbing, a new well, and about three grand for new farm equipment. Dad would still be commuting to Detroit for a few years, Milt was off to college, so the bulk of the farm work was done by Dad, Grandpa Joe, Dave, and me. Yep, with the help of friends, many purchases at local farm auctions, and good fortune, we got a crop in the first year. We also raised feeder cattle that winter. Dad's dream became reality, even with the terrible commute to Detroit. In hindsight, Mom gave up a lot: Her lovely house in Allen Park, her friends at church, and a village setting for the rural life on a farm. I never thought of it at the time, but she must have loved Dad, to have given up so much.

I embraced farm life, and, in time, would get a horse (more on that later), and grew in new directions, with responsibility that comes with equipment operation, handling animals, and growing/harvesting crops to be profitable.

Get this: Joe and Em liked the farm so much, they built a house there in 1952, and in 1960, when we sold the farm, moved it to a lot on Lake Erie. Now, *that* was an event. I should add, Uncle Del also moved his steam engines and two threshing machines to our farm. Can you imagine how cool it was to fill silo, thrash corn, and pull stumps with Del's engines the way farmers did in the 1800s? There was one drawback. Our chickens molted one month after being scared out of their wits by the very loud steam whistle. Oh well; live and learn. How many guys my age were taught how to start up a steam engine, replace boiler tubes, and the workings of a governor to keep an engine under control? Very few, I'd guess. Also, Duane, Dad's brother, worked on the farm at times.

Wow! What a change in our lives.

No church affiliation, working long hours on the critical need to upgrade the homestead, clearing fields, planting crops, buying equipment and cattle, all while Dad still commuted to Hudson's. He left a few years later, after 25 years, without a retirement package. So he had to work for several local companies, including Mills Bakery in Romulus; Gilman Hardware in Willis; and Lincoln Schools, driving a bus. Mom sure gave up a lot, nevertheless she soldiered on so he could live his dream.

It was clear that the church was no longer a part of their lives even with a Presbyterian church nearby in Milan. I think there were just not enough hours in the day to refurbish the farm and worship, too.

I loved the farm. Dave and I helped Dad do some serious farming from 1950 to 1953. Then, Dave was off to U of M, and Dad's chest x-ray indicated he had lung cancer. We still farmed, but at a lesser volume. Milt, Irene, and David, moved into Em and Joe's house on the farm in '53. That was a blessing for Dad, as he had a chance to enjoy his first grandson. I did, too.

A short reflection here: While I was a graduate student at U of M between 1972 and 1977, my nephew and I met frequently on N. Campus while both of us were taking classes at GG Brown Engineering Building at the same time. What a pleasure to step out of class and have coffee with him years later.

Okay. That's enough background. It was intended to provide a lead into my story of incidents with Dad. Incidents that had an impact on my life, or are treasured, whether rooted in drama or humor. At times I'll refer to Allen Park and other experiences at the farm in Willis.

*   *   *

The surprise that almost wasn't: 1949.

Dad had said I could have a horse when we moved to the farm. One evening, he and a friend pulled into our yard, opened the trunk of the car, and came looking for me. Not knowing, I wandered home, saw the car with its open trunk, and looked in. There it was, a beautiful western style saddle. I looked around and saw no one. Then, in what seemed like hours, Dad appeared, and said, "There you are. What have you found? See anything interesting?" You can guess the rest. I cried, lifted the horsey-smelling saddle out of the trunk and carried it into my room; I slept with it for days. That didn't last long, though. To store it, I built a wooden horse in the basement, saddle-soaped it every week, and waited for my horse. That all happened about 2 years later. My own dream had come true.

*   *   *

The horse that almost wasn't: 1951.

Our cattle buyer, Honey Konchel, was selling his horse, located on a pasture in Ann Arbor. Honey, Dad, brother Dave, and I maneuvered and chased the beautiful gelding for several hours without success one Sunday afternoon. Honey finally said, "If we don't corral him on this try, let's give up and try another day." Dad and I took the challenge, and darned if we didn't run our legs off. We were successful on that last try. When corralled, the pinto looked even better. Yep, you're right. For the next few months I curried, fed, watered, and rode Chico as the proud new cowboy on the farm. Needless to say, I talked to him every night before bedtime.

*   *   *

Another animal in my life was Fritz, a beautiful, smart, liver-colored German shorthaired pointer, who died in 1952.

Fritz roamed the acreage with few restrictions over the years.

However, one evening he laid down, unable to walk. Dad determined he had some gastrointestinal problem and called the vet. Much to our surprise and shock, he said he could not save him—due to a poison that had a head start on treatment.

"Please try," I cried.

Dad said it was too late. Unable to handle the event, I climbed up to the top of the silo, sat in the ensilage, and cried. Why there? I didn't want my emotions to show.

After a short search, Dad appeared and sat with me, and explained how normal it is to cry. Even he cried. He also chatted about the good times with Fritz while hunting. He promised to get another dog—not like Fritz, but similar. That's the way life is, he said. We live, we love, we die. And, yes, we cry at times. It's normal. He ended the session with a little humor, saying, "Remember when you were hunting with him and the group, and you emptied your shotgun at a bird without a feather touched? We all laughed at the blazing youth, but Fritz did not. He came to your side as if volunteering to flush another bird for you."

With that, I laughed, and we climbed down from the silo.

While walking back to the house, Dad related another similar story about Fritz. "Remember in Allen Park, about three years ago, when we caught you boys smoking in the underground fort? Who do you think caught you? It wasn't me, it was Fritz. He dug up the cigarettes and brought them to me."

"Dang dog," I said. "You made us smoke cigars until we puked."

Dad said, "But you never smoked again."

"Good dog," I said.

We both smiled and related the stories with Mom.

*   *   *

Here's another hunting story that involved our family doctor, Lee Hielman.

Dad and Lee were going to drive a forty-acre plot together, when out of nowhere, Lee says, "Ron, we'll drive the plot with the dogs, you get the car and drive it to the other end.

I looked at Dad. I'd never driven anything other than our John Deere tractor. The car was a new '49 Ford. I'm only 13. I paused. Lee said, "Ron can do it. I've seen him drive the tractor.

Dad nodded.

I felt ten feet tall. It worked out okay, easy as eating pie. Thanks, Dad, for giving me the go-ahead.

*   *   *

Here's an odd one. My first time in a bar—with Dad. 1950.

We had blown an outboard motor on a boat while visiting one of the Jones boys. After dropping it off for repair, one of the Jones boys—Donnie, I think—Dad, and I had to kill time downtown. As we walked toward town, Donnie spotted a bar. He said, "Let's grab a beer and sandwich while we wait." Dad gave me a quick look, as if saying, "Hey, I have my son with me." But Dad must have felt no harm would come. It was noon, and the drinking crowd didn't arrive until later. Well, I sat drinking my Coke in the dark atmosphere of the bar. My eyes were aglow. Dang, so this is what it's like to drink. The music was loud country and western, and the jokes were a little risqué. However, guess who had grown up real quick, I thought, as I bragged to my buddies. Later, Dad mentioned that he, too, did not drink away from home, and if Donnie did, fine, but it's not a good idea to do—unless it's a special occasion, like TV on a sporting event not covered at home.

*   *   *

A surprise visit from one of Dad's friends, Ivan Galpin. 1954.

I had worked on Sam Parker's farm a couple of weeks, in 1953. He was Irene's dad, a good friend. At that time, I met Ivan, who helped Sam.

I'm not sure if Dad and Mom knew Ivan and his wife were coming, but he came with an offer to live and work for him, as a hired hand, at $125 a month, for three months, on his farm. He had 60 head of cattle, milked 40, and farmed 160 acres in Ann Arbor. Seems his former hired hand had run off with a wild woman one night. Holy cow! I couldn't just leave the farm and place the burden on Dave—especially with Dad sick from his treatments. Apparently they had already had that discussion, and it was up to me to decide. I looked at Dad for help, and it came quickly with a short walk. He said he and Dave could handle the farm since all the crops were in and harvesting was the only task ahead.

It turned out to be a great move. I learned a lot, and I loved the Galpin family. They really appreciated my decision. In fact, their daughter, Sue, named her first child after me. I left in late August for football practice and thanked everyone, especially Dad, for the late summer's activities.

*   *   *

Finally. Buying my first car with Dad. 1953.

At 16, I'd sold my 4-H steer for $400 and was permitted to look for a car. I found a cool, souped-up '40 Ford with shaved heads and racing tires. Needless to say, when I showed the rod to Dad, he disapproved (wisely so), and I was upset. Then, about a week later, he said, "Get your four hundred together, we're going to get you a car." Unbeknownst to me, he'd been looking and found a '46 Ford at a dealer's lot in Romulus, where he worked. On the way, he said, "Here's the deal. They want five hundred, but you pull out the four hundred and say that's all you have. Don't forget to mention it's from selling your steer." In short, we closed the deal at $400, and with Dad's effort, got a tank of gas and a grease job—something I would have never thought of. Yep,

I learned a lot that day about being patient and how to close a deal that's most favorable to the buyer.

*   *   *

Dad died in the summer of '55, and I stayed with Mom on the farm for the next five years while getting a college degree. We sold the farm in 1960.

There's many more stories but let's cut it short with these six. I've tried to relate some aspects of Dad's personality as he worked with me. If you'd like to hear more, let's talk. Have you drawn the same conclusion I have? I'm blessed to have known Dad.

MISTAKEN IDENTITY

An Essay

To many engineers, and scientists, space exploration in the sixties and seventies was referred to as the Golden Years. The close knit team of designers and managers had met President Kennedy's

1961 challenge to "Go to the moon and return safely in this dec-ade." Some think this goal was triggered by the Russians orbiting Sputnik as it *beeped* annoyingly while passing over U.S. receivers.

Due to this challenge, NASA was formed, a team assembled, and through a series of programs—beginning with Mercury, then Gemini, and finally Apollo—six of seven planned flights took off and safely returned. From Apollo 11 landing on July 20, 1969 to Apollo 17 touching down on December 7, 1972, many contrac-tors provided NASA managers with hundreds of talented design-ers, engineers, and testing personnel. That's where my story begins, in what I call *Mistaken Identity*. Due to my age, size, physi-cal condition, and flight training, I was selected as the design, test, and evaluation engineer—sometimes referred to as *half astronaut*. Why such a name? I was trained in much the same field as actual flight crews. That training included operations in the Block 2 space suit, vacuum chamber survival, passing a class two aviator physical, zero and 1/6 gravity simulation in water as well as in the G-Force One—also known as the vomit comet—aircraft at Wright Patterson Air Force Base, and familiarity with collimated light (in the vacuum of the moon, a shadow is absolute black).

This is where my story starts, as I show how I fit into this once-in-a-lifetime program of space exploration.

There were three contractors that designed hardware for as-tronaut operations. North America worked on the command module; Grumman Corp handled the lunar module; and Bendix dealt with lunar experiments.

My job as the Bendix designer/test evaluation engineer, hav-ing a background in Human Factors—also called Ergonomics—is defined as designing within acceptable limits of a person's abil-ities to ensure success for that task. I was to provide support to the principle investigators and designers, and to evaluate that de-sign *prior* to its introduction to the astronauts; in my (Bendix) case, performing tasks on the lunar surface. The lunar surface design criteria was the most complex due to all the tasks being outside of the lunar module in the hostile environment of the moon. This means no handholds, 1/6 gravity, and collimated light. At sixty pounds with a high center of gravity, the crew member cannot lean over more than thirty degrees. A fall forward would be catastrophic. So each member had a 24 inch handling tool to perform tasks near the surface. This was a constant battle with designers to remind them to require that no task had to be performed near the surface unless a tool was provided.

Enough about design constraints due to suited operations at 1/6 gravity, my unique story is about traveling by commercial air with my NASA space suit.

In early 1968, on a flight from Detroit to Houston, with a stopover in Chicago, I had witnessed the suit going into the plane's cargo bay, per NASA requirements. NASA regulations require visual contact with the suit at all times when traveling by land, sea, or air. I stood on the flight line when it was loaded and would do so in Houston when unloaded. This is not unusual; pilots and airport managers are aware of this requirement for expensive or classified cargo.

However, upon landing at Chicago, a mechanical problem changed our stopover to a plane change—which is not a good thing.

Quickly, I headed to the flight line. I had to witness the transfer of the suit to the new plane. Way ahead of me, the pilot had alerted the cargo crew, and when I arrived at the flight line, they were waiting for me with the transfer cart and a sedan.

However, a strange second crew had gathered by the cart.

Much to my chagrin, it was a group of newspaper reporters. From the logos on their hats and coats they appeared to be from the Tribune, Daily, and other places of which I was unfamiliar. I tried to duck and weave to the sedan, but failed. Before I could slip around the cart, lights came on and cameras started to roll as microphones appeared in my face. Questions were thrust into the air in a cocktail of emotions.

"Where are you headed?"

"Is that really a space suit?"

"Do you think women will be allowed to fly as astronauts?"

"What flight are you on?"

"Would you show us the space suit?"

"Are you married?"

I could not walk away. I was trapped.

"Please," I said. "I'm not an astronaut, but I'll answer a few questions in regards to the Apollo Program."

I explained my role as a Bendix engineer, evaluating several experiments for the flight crew on Apollo Eleven. I'd told them about being the half astronaut, and using Buzz Aldrin's backup suit for this particular test.

"I'm just a Bendix employee doing his job," I explained, climbing into the sedan.

Much to my surprise, a late arrival started in on the same types of questions, and I politely begged off as we drove away.

"Geez," I said to my driver, "I wonder how that crew knew about our transfer of the suit."

"*Your* transfer," he chuckled. "You're an astronaut—as far as those on the base operations frequency are concerned. You didn't stand a chance to remain anonymous."

As we approached the new aircraft, I thought it may be a good idea to stay in the car and watch them load from there. It worked for a moment—until one crew member tapped on the window and asked for an autograph. I signed: Bendix half astronaut.

Finally I arrived at the plane and took my seat.

The stewardess said, "Welcome aboard. We've upgraded you to first class."

I tried to explain that I wasn't an astronaut.

"I know," she said. "But we've put you through a hassle today.

You earned the upgrade."

I settled into my seat and closed my eyes for a moment.

A second stewardess appeared and placed a placard that read *Occupied* on the seat next to me.

"I don't mind sitting beside other travelers," I admitted.

She grinned, lowered her voice, and said, "*You* don't mind, but there are quite a few who just want to sit here with you and chat about your work."

I thanked her for her wisdom and figured that was that.

"But there's a boy," she added. "He'd like an autograph—if you don't mind."

The young fellow stood by my seat, asked a few questions, proffered his boarding pass for me to sign.

He didn't care that I wasn't an actual astronaut.

With a grin on his face, the boy dashed up the aisle to his parents.

I know people meant no harm. My experience was simply a reflection of their pride in NASA's program, the people in it, no matter their job title.

MISSION CONTROL

An Essay

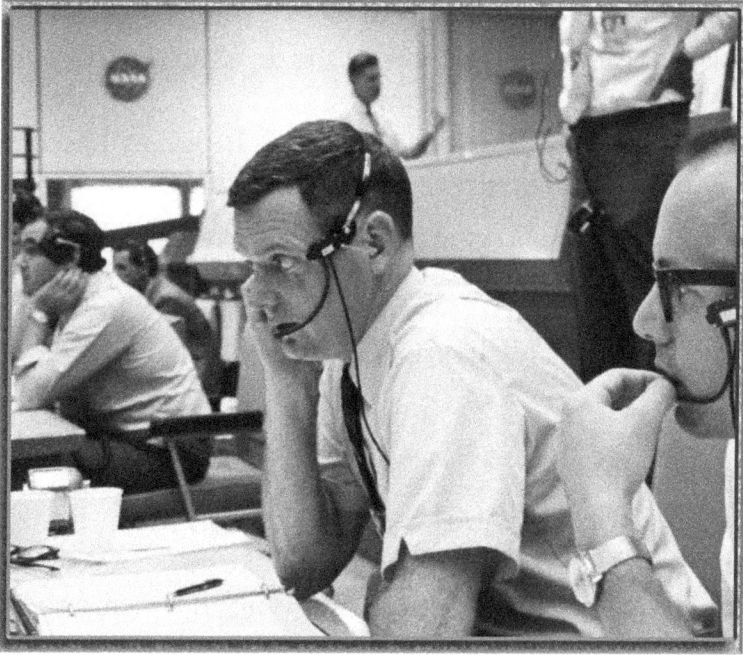

Location: Houston, Texas, NASA Manned Spacecraft Center (MSC) Mission Control

Time: 2030 HRS EST, July 20, 1969

Flight: Apollo #11 has landed successfully on the lunar surface.

In a huge room, dozens of engineers and scientists hover over their consols as the Apollo 11 crew start removing the two experiments from the Lunar Module and begin to orient them on the surface. At one of the critical consols, Capsule Communicator

(CAPCOM) astronaut Charlie Duke is talking to Buzz Aldrin as he attempts to level the Passive Seismometer on the powder-like surface. (Neil Armstrong deploys his experiment nearby.)

The dialog between CAPCOM and Buzz is getting a little stressful:

Charlie: "What did you say? What's wrong?"

Buzz: "Darn it! The BeeBee on the leveling device won't stop spinning around the outside rim!"

Charlie asks Chuck, the Bendix (Bx) Program Director, and me, Bx Crew Trainer, sitting next to him in Mission Control, to slide over and get ready to be involved—remembering very well that all contractor communications for the crew must be relayed through the CAPCOM. As we were moving over to Charlie:

Buzz: "Darn it! This BeeBee on the leveling device won't stop spinning. . .

Hearing the down-link comments, Chuck suggests I move closer to Charlie.

Charlie: (Shooting a look at me.) "Got any ideas, Ron?"

Buzz: (Garbled down-link sounded like . . .) "Ask Ron if this thing, this BeeBee, will ever stop spinning. It never was this bad in training."

Ron to Charlie: "Tell him it will stop spinning, but due to the effects of reduced gravity, it will take longer to find center."

Charlie: "Be patient—"

Buzz: "Ahhh, it stopped and rolled to the center and stayed. . . that means it must be level, right?"

Charlie looks at me. I nod in the affirmative.

Charlie: "You're good. It just takes a little longer in reduced gravity. Good show. You're good to go."

Buzz: "Okay, off to geology. Here I come, Neil."

Neil, busy deploying the Laser Ranging Retro Reflector (LRRR) nearby, finishes his tasks and joins Buzz in their geologic tasks collecting rocks.

Charlie and I retreat to the contractors' support room to stand by until mission completion, as always, hoping for the crew's safe return. Personally, I'm seeing white smoke from the chimney.

*   *   *

What's this all about? Many of you may not have been around or watched the lunar landing on July 20, 1969, and may be asking why an astronaut and a contractor are so involved in the deployment of lunar experiments. Let me explain.

The first word that comes to mind is designing tasks to *unknowns*.

Sure, after the fact, we know the surface is like a powder about 1-2 inches deep, and the pressurized space suit worked well in the reduced gravity. But, we did *not* know very much about the surface and how well the suit would perform in pre-mission planning.

The second part of the unknowns was my job. Just how much could we ask the crew to do in a pressurized space suit? To the best of our ability, we had to simulate lunar surface operations, so the crew would be successful and safe, while deploying experiments.

We learned a lot about suited crew capabilities during the Mercury and Gemini programs in the early and mid-1960s. However, the unknown lunar surface presented new challenges. Let me present a few of the test and evaluation tasks we performed to ensure success.

*   *   *

Through accidental timing and age, plus my design work in Human Factors in the U. S. Army (airborne communications equipment), I began work at Bendix Aerospace Systems Division in Ann Arbor in 1965. Lucky for me, I immediately started the astronaut training program at NASA's training facilities in Houston, TX, Wright Patterson Air Force Base (WPAFB) Ohio, MIRAMAR Naval Air Station, S. D., CA. I was just about the right size, in good shape, and passed the aviator grade flight physical, so I was on my way. To do what, you may ask.

My primary mission was to ensure the crew deployment of Bx built experiments were constructed within the constraints of the pressurized suit in reduced gravity. That's it.

But to do so I had to experience reduced weight in Force One (the vomit comet), vacuum chamber work, water immersion tank conditions, and determine just how much tactile feel a crew has while in the pressurized suit. Furthermore, how far forward can the crew be asked to lean before falling over—which for safety reasons is not allowed. Then there's collimated light problems on the moon. Yep, where there is no atmosphere to reflect light in a lunar shadow, it is ebony black.

To do all this evaluation, we formed a Human Factors Group (HFG) and Laboratory, to build models of the experiments and fabricate a portion of the Lunar Module (LM) that housed the Bx experiments, as well as fabricate a best guess, lunar surface of fine beach sand.

NASA also loaned us Jim Irwin's Blk II Apollo space suit since he and I had the same general physical size. That's about all the likeness we shared. He kidded me frequently as a high performance test pilot (having tested the Lockheed SR-71) and I was learning to fly a little Cessna 172. The Blackbird was supersonic at 2.5 mach, and the Cessna 172 in a tail wind 70 mph. Jim, a great guy, flew later successfully on Apollo 15. I can't remember how many times when I'd ask what time is was, he'd say (in Yogi Berra fashion) "You mean, right now?"

In 1966, Bx was awarded a multiyear contract to design, fabricate, test, and deliver all the experiments for lunar exploration from Apollo 11 to 18. (You may remember, 18 was cancelled due to funding and other political reasons.) Over the next two years, several models were assigned to Bx, the first five for Apollo 11. Many models were tested. The Engineering unit (functional but not to form), Qualifications unit (form and function for stress tests), Crew Trainer for Human Factors test (us) the NASA crew trainer, and, finally, the Flight unit (which would be the frozen design headed to the moon).

Many individual experiments were also built by the HF lab to evaluate reduced gravity in water and in Force One at WPAFB.

Let me share with you one of the constant problems that the experiment designers overlooked:

Simply put: *Center of Gravity* changes in the suit and a very light foothold on the surface.

First, the suit and backpack only weighed 60 pounds on the moon (360 on earth) and that weight shifted on the body up about a foot and back about six inches. As such, a crew member *cannot* be asked to perform a task that requires leaning forward beyond 30 degrees. Of course, if required, I'd have to remind the designer that a handling tool 24 inches long must be used. That was a terrible burden to some. But they came up with a design, I tested it, and in most cases, the unique astronaut handling tool did the job. If a handling task was rejected time and time again, I just asked the designer to attend a test, and then the problem was viewed objectively. None of them wanted their experiment beat up during deployment. Most of them treated their experiment as an extension of themselves. There's nothing wrong with that, since the crew felt the same way.

Part of our HF tasks were to determine the *time line* for deploying experiments.

That's when the first serious timing problem raised its ugly head.

On the first flight, Apollo 11, we were constrained by the Extravehicular Activity (EVA) time of only 1 ½ hours for experiment deployment and geology.

The bad news: Our first Lunar Package called ALSEP (Apollo Lunar Surface Experiment Package) contained five experiments requiring 45 minutes to deploy.

That caused a problem. The powers that be at NASA wanted the major portion of lunar surface activity to be in geologic exploration and collection. As a result, we were directed to design an alternative package that would have only two passive experiments and took only 15 minutes to deploy.

It would be called EASEP (Early Apollo Surface Experiment Package).

Now, everyone was happy—except Bendix.

For Bendix it meant 10-12 hour days, 7 days a week, to meet NASA schedule requirements. We had to deliver a flight unit in six months that would normally take 12 on units that were on the cutting edge of design.

The modified (hurry up) program developed in January 1969, looked like this:

- Fabricate engineering, qualification, and crew models at the same time.
- Gain astronaut approval with an extensive test and evaluation program.
- Hold a Design Review with NASA engineers, management, and crew.
- Have crew handle actual flight model at KSC.
- Launch.
- Land on lunar surface and deploy on July 20, 1969.
- CAPCOM/Bx Team provide support in Mission Control while crew is on the moon.

That's where we stepped in. . . to page one. . . and I'll step out.

ABOUT THE AUTHOR

Mark Allen North

Michigan native Mark Allen North is a retired aerospace engineer, industrialist, and educator who has published many technical and academic articles, primarily in the field of human-factors design. Now he is a novelist and writer of short stories and personal-experience essays. He is a longtime student of Native American spirituality, which led him to pen his first three novels, The Lady Trilogy.

Fresh Ink Group

Publishing
Free Memberships
Share & Read Free Stories, Essays, Articles
Free-Story Newsletter
Writing Contests
❧
Books
E-books
Amazon Bookstore
❧
Authors
Editors
Artists
Professionals
Publishing Services
Publisher Resources
❧
Members' Websites
Members' Blogs
Social Media

www.FreshInkGroup.com
Email: info@FreshInkGroup.com
Twitter: @FreshInkGroup
Google+: Fresh Ink Group
Facebook.com/FreshInkGroup
LinkedIn: Fresh Ink Group
About.me/FreshInkGroup

Fresh Ink Group

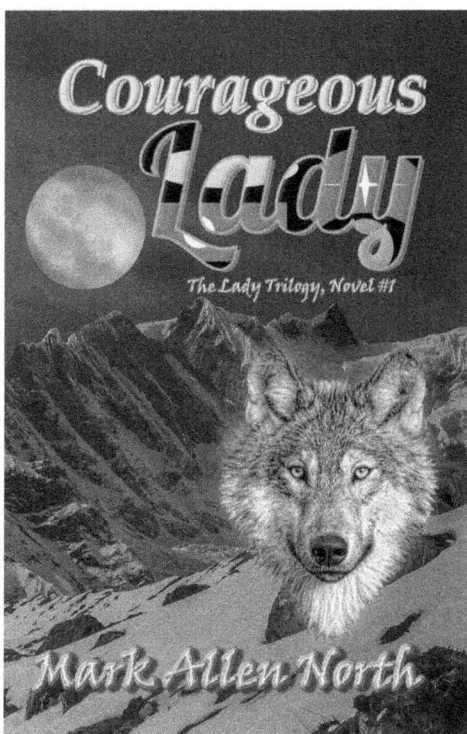

Courageous Lady

The Lady Trilogy, Novel #1

Mark Allen North

In the first novel of The Lady Trilogy, auburn-haired Leigh West travels to Alaska's majestic and mysterious Tongass National Forest in search of self-discovery and harmony with nature. In her journal, she chronicles all she learns from native Tlingit tribesmen and nature: the cunning wolves, belligerent brown bears, and those transforming seasons of the region's glorious landscape. It is through Native American spirituality that she sparks new passion within herself, a new appreciation for the physical world, and a life filled with love.

www.FreshInkGroup.com

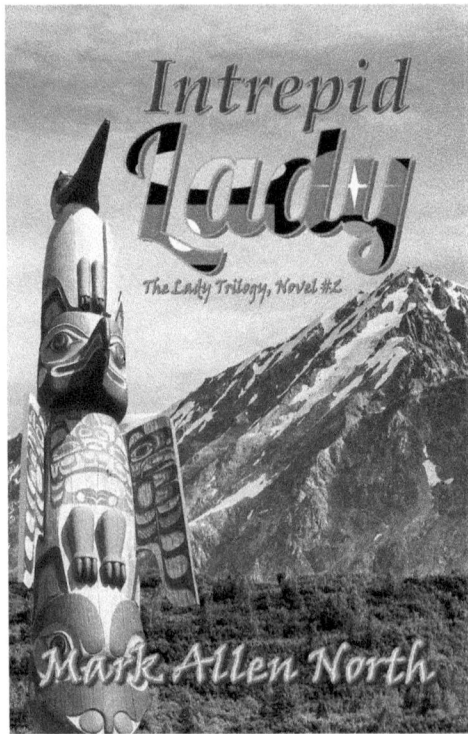

Intrepid Lady
The Lady Trilogy, Novel #2
Mark Allen North

In the second novel of The Lady Trilogy, auburn-haired beauty Leigh West continues her adventures in Alaska's majestic and mysterious Tongass National Forest in search of self-discovery and harmony with nature. In her journal, she chronicles becoming the Spiritual wife of Chi Mukwa (Big Bear) and guardian of two Tlingit teens. It is through Native American spirituality that she sparks new passion within herself, a new appreciation for others, and a life filled with love.

www.FreshInkGroup.com

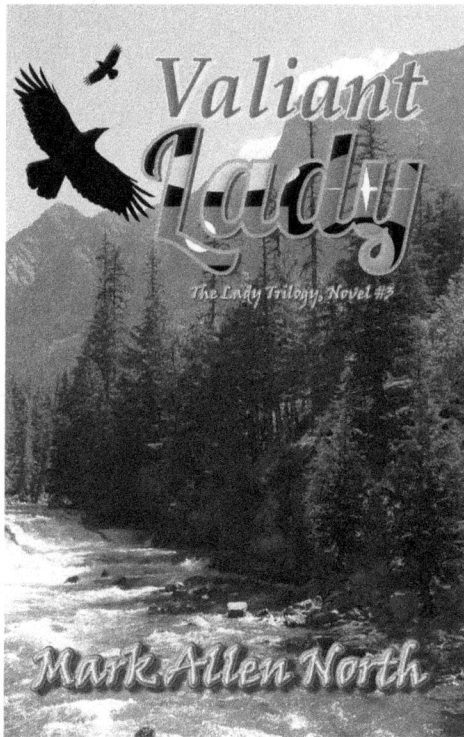

In the third novel of The Lady Trilogy, auburn-haired beauty Leigh West continues her adventures in Alaska's majestic and mysterious Tongass National Forest in search of self-discovery and harmony with nature. In her journal, she chronicles all she learns from native Tlingit tribesmen. She marries one and adopts two, fights fire with vigor, and promotes environmental concerns all in the transforming seasons of the region's glorious landscape. It is through Native American spirituality that she sparks new passion within herself, a new appreciation for the physical world, and a life filled with love.

www.FreshInkGroup.com

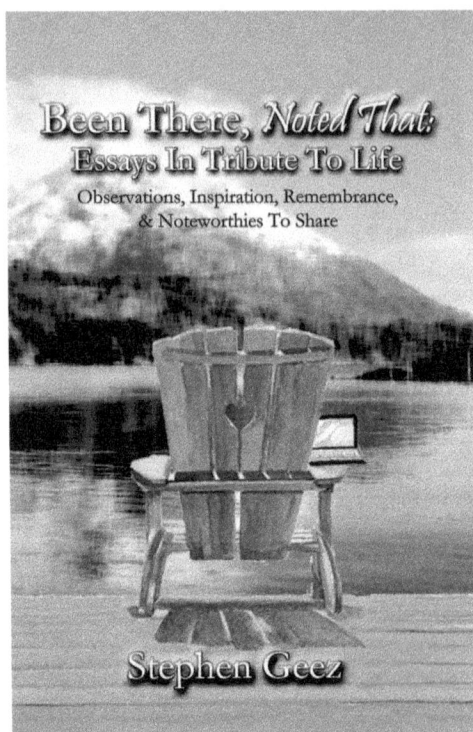

Been There, *Noted That:*
Essays In Tribute To Life
Observations, Inspiration, Remembrance,
& Noteworthies To Share

Stephen Geez

The simple lives of everyday people in a mundane world prove extraordinary in this collection of 54 personal-experience essays by novelist Stephen Geez. The eclectic mix of memoir, commentary, humor, and appreciation covers a wide range of topics, each beautifully illustrated by artists and photographers from the Fresh Ink Group. Geez catches what many of us miss, then considers how we might all share the most poignant of lessons. *Been There, Noted That* aims to reveal who we are, examine where we've been, and discover what we dare strive to become.

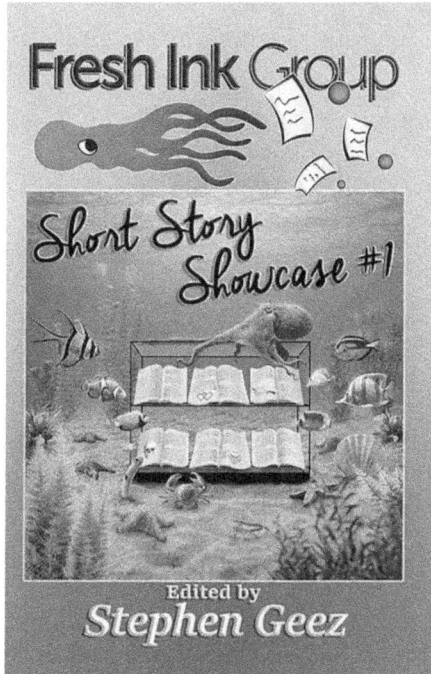

Fresh Ink Group showcases 42 compelling prize-winners from its literary and genre short-story contests. Eclectic, daring, subtle, provocative, diverse—this wide-ranging collection by authors from across the USA and around the world transcends the limits of single-theme anthologies to explore the best of many styles and bold new ideas. Travel through time and space. Experience the southern-farm snake, suicidal love lost, politicians run amok, a serial killer's lair, seductive sorcerous charms, a malevolent-house warning, inevitable moon-base death, the vengeful walking corpse, or a Holocaust child's hope, the lament of a life never lived . . . Discerning story-lovers are invited to listen for the voices of these newly favorite authors in *Fresh Ink Group Short Story Showcase #1*.

www.FreshInkGroup.com

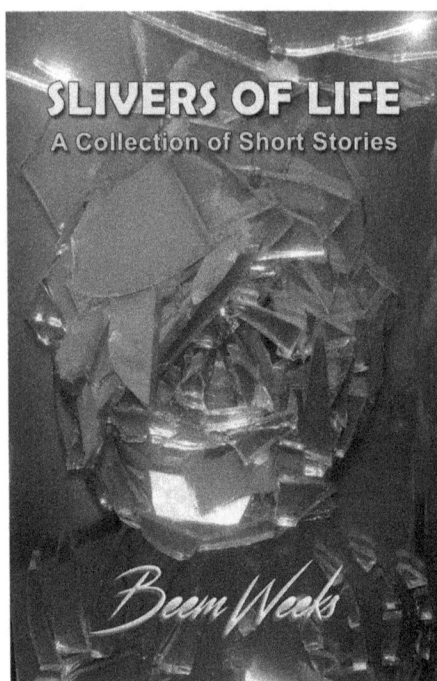

SLIVERS OF LIFE
A Collection of Short Stories

Beem Weeks

These twenty short stories are a peek into individual lives caught up in spectacular moments in time. Children, teens, mothers, and the elderly each have stories to share. Readers witness tragedy and fulfillment, love and hate, loss and renewal. Historical events become backdrops in the lives of ordinary people, those souls forgotten with the passage of time. Beem Weeks tackles diverse issues running the gamut from Alzheimer's disease to civil rights, abandonment to abuse, from young love to the death of a child. Long-hidden secrets and notions of revenge unfold at the promptings of rich and realistic characters; plot lines often lead readers into strange and dark corners. Within *Slivers of Life*, Weeks proves that everybody has a story to tell—and no two are ever exactly alike.

www.FreshInkGroup.com

www.ingramcontent.com/pod-product-compliance
Lightning Source LLC
Chambersburg PA
CBHW021926040426
42448CB00008B/931